The Meaning of These Days

The Meaning of These Days

Memoir of a Philosophical Pastor

KENNETH D. STEPHENS

RESOURCE *Publications* • Eugene, Oregon

THE MEANING OF THESE DAYS
Memoir of a Philosophical Pastor

Copyright © 2013 Kenneth D. Stephens. All rights reserved. Except for brief quotations in critical publications or reviews, no part of this book may be reproduced in any manner without prior written permission from the publisher. Write: Permissions, Wipf and Stock Publishers, 199 W. 8th Ave., Suite 3, Eugene, OR 97401.

Resource Publications
An Imprint of Wipf and Stock Publishers
199 W. 8th Ave., Suite 3
Eugene, OR 97401
www.wipfandstock.com

ISBN 13: 978-1-62032-814-9
Manufactured in the U.S.A.

In memory of my father,
the Rev. Daniel K. Stephens

Contents

	Preface	*xi*
	Prologue	1
1	Connaught Place *It was plain I was good for only one thing: religion*	3
2	Mt. Tamalpais *Listening to the night sounds of San Francisco in Montgomery Hall*	8
3	Sacred Ground *Buber's simple thoughts stream from the page into the understanding*	13
4	Market Street *If you're young, take a chance if you love her*	16
5	Yosemite Valley *I sat down by the river and read*	20
6	Tioga Pass *My Barth volumes go missing on the way to Tuolumne Meadows*	24
7	The Scream *Niebuhr cast his net far and wide over human experience*	28
8	Los Angeles *In the wee small hours of the morning*	33
9	Mount Baldy *The courage to be in the face of nonbeing*	37

10 Chapter Zero   42
    Lemmon was high-powered and driven,
    Louch grounded and relaxed

11 Kierkegaard's Truth   47
    I go to be hanged on yonder gallows

12 Kurukshetra   51
    They've given you a number, and taken 'way your name

13 The Tahquamenon   55
    I will arise and go now, and go to Innisfree

14 Springer Mountain   59
    Consciousness III was blowing in the wind

15 Peachtree Street   63
    I cover the waterfront, I'm watching the sea

16 Atlanta   69
    The person of heaven gives to the person of dust a prayer

17 Stone Mountain   74
    There's a fire softly burning, supper's on the stove

18 The Narraguagus   78
    I eat of the tree of the knowledge of good and evil

19 The Berkshires   84
    Deception and truth walked hand in hand on the village green

20 Gotham City   89
    I'll come running to see you again

21 The Hudson   94
    Archbishop Oscar Romero had just been assassinated

22 Puget Sound   98
    Comfort the sorrowing and stand in solidarity
    with the weak and powerless

23	Middle Path *Moth and rust corrupted and thieves broke through to steal*	104
24	Mount Rainier *A voice said, Cry! and I said, What shall I cry?*	109
25	The Whirlwind *'Tis seven long years since last I've seen you*	113
26	Nein! *I said to my soul, be still, and let the dark come upon you*	120
27	The Tower *To which dost thou belong? Spirit or nature?*	125
28	The Uncompahgre *Please come back to a heart that is true*	128
29	Blue Oaks *I myself arrive in the valley of dry bones*	134
30	Buffalo Rock *I do best when I'm not alone*	138
31	Landour *Walking tall on Main Street in the May Day parade*	144

Preface

THIS BOOK STARTED AS a tract in philosophical theology after I left my profession as an academic philosopher and began my work as a pastor. Soon it turned into this memoir, in which I was able to write how philosophy and religion interacted in the joys and travails of my personal and pastoral life. In this form the book gathered a certain literary significance and a novelistic appeal for seekers, pilgrims, and lost souls on diverse paths and no-paths.

Indeed the book, having been written intermittently over the last thirty years of my ministry, came of age trying to come to grips with the two extremes of the contemporary spiritual quandary. The one side was expressed by Jane Kramer recently, writing in The New Yorker, that we live in fierce theological times. She was referring to Islamic radicalism, its reproach of Western decadence and secularism, and its espousal of its own religious absolutism and exclusivism. She said this surely knowing that Christian fundamentalism thrives on the same critique and narrowmindedness. The other side is the assault we are witnessing on religion itself by some of its cultured despisers, a term used early in the twentieth century by the great liberal theologian Friederich Schleiermacher.

Among the many friends to whom I owe thanks for help and encouragement in the writing of my manuscript are John Cobb, Jr. and Gilchrist McLaren. Cobb is the world-renowned process theologian in Claremont, California. He became my seminary teacher in 1961 and has been my friend ever since. McLaren has been my friend since my college days in India. I found the suggestions of Judy Rollins, a superb writer in her own right, very helpful indeed. Thanks to her and to Connie Kimos for editing this work in such a perceptive, thoughtful, and sensitive way. She was also kind in her personal remarks, generously given along the way.

I have changed some names and details in order to protect people from what might be taken as aspersions on their character, though no such slights are ever intended.

KDS

Prologue

From Henry Van Dyke's Classic Story of *The Other Wise Man*

In the days when Augustus Caesar was master of many kings and Herod reigned in Jerusalem, there lived in the city of Ecbatana, among the mountains of Persia, a certain man named Artaban, the Median. His house stood close to the outermost of the seven walls which encircled the royal treasury. From his house he could look over the rising battlements of black and white and crimson and blue and red and silver and gold, to the hill where the summer palace of the Parthian emperors glittered like a jewel in a sevenfold crown.

Around the dwelling of Artaban spread a fair garden, a tangle of flowers and fruit trees, watered by a score of streams descending from the slopes of Mount Orontes, and made musical by innumerable birds. But all color was lost in the soft and odorous darkness of the late September night, and all sounds were hushed in the deep charm of its silence, save the plashing of the water, like a voice half-sobbing and half-laughing under the shadows. High above the trees a dim glow of light shone through the curtained arches of the upper chamber, where the master of the house was holding council with his friends.

He stood by the doorway to greet his guests—a tall, dark man of about forty years, with brilliant eyes set near together under his broad brow, and firm lines graven around his fine, thin lips; the brow of a dreamer and the mouth of a soldier, a man of sensitive feeling but inflexible will— one of those who, in whatever age they may live, are born for inward conflict and a life of quest.

1

Connaught Place

It was plain I was good for only one thing, religion

She was a pretty Japanese woman looking at me with a faint smile. It was in a small café, and I was probably drinking chai, tea with cream and sugar, I do not remember. She was standing at an entrance to the back rooms, and from my angle of vision I could see only what may have looked like a booth for the café's customers. She was about my age, twenty. There had been other waitresses just a while ago, but now in a glass darkly I see just her and me. Together they may have decided that she was the right one. No word was spoken.

It was at the port of Tokyo, and the year was 1957. The President Cleveland was waiting in the Harbor. I had flown Pan American from Calcutta to Hong Kong, and had boarded the ship there. Here we were given a few hours. I had time.

The temptation was real but I actually had no intention of yielding. There could be danger in the back rooms, or the maze of back rooms. A man could appear and hover over me with a knife. He would demand my money, or worse, my papers. He would see a hapless, innocent, boyish man sitting on the bed with the pretty woman, but that would not soften him.

There was yet another reason why I said No to the temptation, and I write this with my younger pilgrim readers especially in mind. The act would be an impossible burden for a young person in mid-voyage to carry. The wages of sin is death, says Paul in Romans, and I heard Albrecht

The Meaning of These Days

Durer's horsemen Sin and Death, already prowling, come up from behind. Sin strikes first, injecting the victim with the venom. Then the purple twilight descends, frightening the victim. Here I was on the threshold of a new dispensation, an opportunity to go to America to find a foothold on life and flourish. This act would put me instead in the ring with Death.

I do not remember what happened next, except that I abstained. Through the mist of time hazily I see me climbing the white stairs up the side of the immense ship and showing my papers to the men in white uniforms. I was safe.

Pilgrim, you should know a bit about my background before you star trek with me to explore unknown worlds, discover new ways of being, and go where no one has ever gone before. Since I was seven I was sent away to English, American, and Anglo-Indian missionary boarding schools in the Himalayan first range, which by trains with their coolies and crowded platforms and compartments, and by buses with their sherpas in their mountain terminals, may as well have been thousands of miles away from my home in the Punjab, and where in time my behavior became rebellious and I became a transgressor. The narrow-gauge train up to Simla and the buses to Mussoorie took sharp curves, went through tunnels and changes of vegetation and climate, and looked down steeply on worlds left behind. The landscape changed rapidly and grew awesome and frightening as we ascended, a foreshadowing of things to come. Every spring it was numbingly traumatic, both the long tear-suppressed ride up with my beloved Aunt Ta, whose silent sadness seemed bottomless, and her dreaded departure when the boy clung to his aunt's sari.

The structure in the schools and the friendships I formed in class and on the playground went a long way to sustain me. A conversion experience brought comfort, stability, and meaning to my life. The missionaries from all over the world would bring their Bibles to the services in Kellogg Church on top of Landour mountain. From there we could see both the eternal snows to the north and the sweltering plains to the south far below. On that sacred site at the age of eleven I knew what I too was good for.

But I failed my BA exams at St. Stephens College in Delhi. I was on my own in New Delhi on Parliament Street and ill-prepared for this new life and brand of education in the big city. My personal life had lost whatever grounding and skeleton it had had in the boarding schools with their dormitory life, their joint study and dining, their sports team and camaraderie with teachers and friends. My father lived with me, but he was himself a solitary figure, frequently gone. Pilgrim, I do not do well when I am alone.

One day my father and I were bicycling back from a meal at my Aunt Dorothy's small apartment in Gol Market, where my mother and younger brother and some in-laws also lived. At the entrance to a bazaar he told me his side of the back story with my mother. Amid the bustle of bicycle and motor rickshaws and taxis and pedestrians, a shameful family secret was told. It was the lightning flash that brought everything into focus. My father was giving me the key to the world. It was painful for him to share it, and it was impossible for me to hear it. By then I had learned to live with the order that had emerged without asking questions.

On all accounts New Delhi was the place to be at midcentury soon after independence. I experienced those Jawaharlal Nehru days, however, as a disjointed figure gawking from outside the gate. The new 1956 Thunderbird was showcased in a window at Connaught Place, part of the elegant British buildings designed by Edwin Lutgens and Herbert Baker in the early 20th century. The jazz combos from Portuguese Goa, featured by some of the night spots, were as good at the standards as any I have ever heard since then. I listened standing at the door, my mind body become a finely tuned instrument vibrating to the romance and rhythm of *Someone to Watch Over Me*. Then and there I was an American GI, handsome and tall and unbeatable like Tab Hunter.

To advertise the movie, the bridge over the river Kwai swung physically across the street to the Regal Cinema. No postmodern disillusion here, but a modernistic private sector optimism about the bridges that can be built, the waters that can be crossed. New winds from the West were sweeping the land. People were talking. The private buzz everywhere was about owning a telephone, air conditioning, a refrigerator, a stereo set. Television was on its way, and cars with the sleek, flashy designs of the brave new world were about to arrive. Cinerama was already here, just around the corner from *The Bridge on the River Kwai*.

The reading room at St. Stephens College was packed every morning, not a spare newspaper or magazine in sight. I watched with admiration and no small envy those wellborn young men with strong families and roots, sons of prominent politicians and successful merchants, who knew exactly what information they needed, where to look for it, and how it could be used to advance their life. The wide-eyed ebullient history professor lectured conversationally, without notes, often looking out the window at the

The Meaning of These Days

Anglican architecture and grassy courtyard as the great Mughal thrones of Babur, Akbar, Jehangir, and Shah Jahan passed by. Nonetheless I had no background or inclination for the subjects I studied, nor did I know how to study them.

Emotionally I was quite close to Aunt Dorothy, who taught at a Christian school close to Gol Market. Sometimes I accompanied her when she went shopping for fabrics and saris in historic Chandni Chowk in Old Delhi, not far from the equally historic Red Fort. Slums and tall dark-looking apartment buildings with brothels extended on both sides of the ancient bazaar. As a family we were socially marginal, though we were deeply religious. Next to the St. Stephens students, however, I felt culturally derelict and psychically uninhabited.

Oh, I tried to put on an upscale front, pleasing to the cultured eye, but it was plain I was good for only one thing, religion. I felt airy, rootless in this big city, and religion was the key to my consolation, the doorway to my survival. Life had been hard enough in the boarding schools. Here anxiety found no harbor, desire could not be patient for the right match, hope scrabbled in vain for a future. Love was unhinged and jealous from the start.

The young woman who waited for me on Parliament Street down below was radiant, vibrant. Love like a vulture reached deep into the core of me, pulling at my bowels. Torrential waves of wanting and jealousy tortured me. I was sinking into a quicksand in an emotional jungle that I did not know. What was happening to me? Was I uncommonly and incorrigibly shy? Was I hobbled by the Himalayan scale of my insecurity? Did I have no maturity or inner strength? Did I mistrust women that profoundly? Was I torn between heart and mind? Did I know intuitively and instinctively the slow simmering secret of love?

I dropped to my knees. It was the re-conversion that calmed the tumultuous sea, just like the first time up at Kellogg Church in Landour. It reconnected me on the inside, gave me a sense of freedom, of strength. It made it easier to navigate the choppy waters of my personal life. With the discipline of prayer and Bible study I was something of a fuller being with more of my faculties in place. An important and innate part of me, whoever or whatever I was, had been missing.

And it was good that I attended the Christian ashram of E. Stanley Jones in the Himalayan foothills with my newfound college friends Gilchrist and Mohit in the summers. The seventy-year-old missionary, writer,

Connaught Place

and silver-tongued preacher and lecturer, dressed in white kameez and dhoti, emboldened me as to what I myself could do and be. His eloquence, conviction, and the transcendent force of his character and message opened up possibilities that I had not imagined.

Back in New Delhi I handed out in Connaught Place the individual Gospels in the form of attractive little booklets. I prayed on the rooftop about the woman I was mad about. My emotions were yet raw. Suddenly I was still a boy standing scared at the edge of the deep country well outside the Railway Hospital in my home town Ferozepore, and I could see the black water far down. I could not understand this bottomless new madness that afflicted me. I took refuge from the abyss in my Bible, marking up the assurances and promises and comforts as Brother Stanley did with his.

In the meantime my father was writing letters, making connections, his eye on the raging sea.

2

Mount Tamalpais

*Listening to the night sounds of
San Francisco in Montgomery Hall*

In Tokyo the foreign student population of the ship got much larger, and on the ocean the diet of soup with noodles got tiresome. To my surprise, none other than Norman Vincent Peale addressed us on Sunday. I had heard of him and other New York City preachers like Harry Emerson Fosdick and George Buttrick in my mid-teens from my father. He had some of their books in his small library when we were living in Ambala, and I think I remember seeing The *Power of Positive Thinking* in that cabinet. I do not remember what Norman Vincent Peale said to the foreign students on the open seas, but it does not matter. I sat riveted. He was a red rubber ball of vitality and inspiration.

    I also remember trying to read Lewis Mumford's *Technics and Civilization* and Reinhold Niebuhr's *The Nature and Destiny of Man*, both of which I found in that cabinet. During World War Two my father had done graduate work at Columbia University and Union Theological Seminary, where he had taken classes with Niebuhr. He would talk frequently about Niebuhr, how knowledgeable he was, and filled with ideas, how effervescent he was in his seminars. And also about New York City, how tall were the skyscrapers and colossal the department stores, where you could buy anything from a safety pin to a battleship.

    My father's name was Daniel Khazan Singh then. During the partition of the country and the horrific religious riots, when he was called back quickly, he and the whole family after him changed our last name to

Mount Tamalpais

Stephens to distinguish ourselves as Christians. Stephen was my grandfather's first name. It was he that was converted by missionaries.

No, Pilgrim, the books by Mumford and Niebuhr were beyond me. I did read E. Stanley Jones' daily devotional books, the most popular among them being *Abundant Life*. I also became engrossed in the Captain Marvel, Superman, and Batman comics which I bought from the English language bookstore. Since I was under age, I tipped the quiet and aloof one-eyed cleaning person to bring me the Scandinavian nudist magazine I had just seen in the shop and keep quiet about it. I gave him a brown paper bag to bring it in.

Ambala had an air force base and an English language movie theater, where I fell in love with Doris Day and waited patiently for movies with Gary Cooper, Montgomery Clift, and Elizabeth Taylor, glossy advertisement photographs and posters of whom were on display in the lobby. Here I saw *An American in Paris*, *A Place in the Sun*, the Tarzan movies, and westerns such as *The Streets of Laredo*, the original one with that title starring William Holden, Macdonald Carey, Mona Freeman, and William Bendix. After sixty years those names come easily to my tongue. The song from *Laredo* lives now only in my head and is heard only in my car. "I was just rambling through/ On the streets of Laredo./ I was just a stranger that day/ On the road to anywhere." The verse I've made up goes something like this: She cried when we woke in *manana*. She knew that soon we'd be parting. She murmured You go Santa Ana, and I to Ol' Mexico.

It is impossible to explain the depth and expanse of the power that these movies had on me. I began to think differently and see myself differently. They made me cry, they made me laugh out loud, they made me sing. They made me a lone and brave warrior. I was a blank tablet for them. My imagination was ablaze. Would I ever grow up out of Hollywood's World War Two dramas and musical comedies?

One day during my winter break my father and I were coming through the gate after a walk, and out of curiosity he reached into my back pocket and pulled out the paperback western *The Valley of Dry Bones* by Arthur Henry Gooden. As we talked he gave me the gut-wrenching news, which I had no choice but to accept: I would not be going back to the American boarding school where I had studied for five years. Instead I would be going to one of the Anglo-Indian schools across the valley, one of the schools against which we competed in sports. They do not want you back, he said, and I cannot afford to send you there anyway.

The Meaning of These Days

Strong bonds of friendships had formed at the American school with Richard, Ray, Ramesh, Jeremy, and many others. I had spent a boyhood there collecting ferns and beetles and chasing butterflies, the exquisite colors gleaming in their bouncy, erratic, unrepeatable flight and in the openings and closings of their wings after they alighted. There were so many species then, and the sightings never ceased to be new discoveries for me. Those creatures were manifestations of the resilient, transitory, and fragmentary nature of the earth's beauty. Furthermore, visions in my head about my being a winner for our sports teams in the interschool Olympics had become part of the reason for my existence.

I also roamed the hillside forest and had secret places in it that were all my own. There was a gentle rhododendron slope with red clay that I loved. There was a shining slope with tall pines and an old abandoned cabin with broken doors in which I loitered. I loved the aroma of the pines and the ground beneath, a thick and soft carpet of pine needles. This second hillside dropped quickly and the trail led down to the stream from Dhobi Ghat, the washers' village, and up the next mountain with a lone tree in the middle of a clearing on the ridge. We could see it clearly every day from Ridgewood, the young boys' dorm. I called it Lone Tree Mountain and dreamed of hiking there someday.

The President Cleveland sailed on to Honolulu, and then when we saw the gull we knew we were approaching the United States mainland. I was met at the port by Ted, a tall, businesslike young man, the treasurer of the student body of San Francisco Theological Seminary in San Anselmo, fifteen miles north of San Francisco. It is set on a hill in the shadow of Mount Tamalpais and its forested slopes. My room was on the second floor of the single men's dormitory, Montgomery Hall, a medieval castle-looking building with ivy on the walls, hardwood floors, and big windows. This would be good for me. I would not be alone here.

Among my classmate friends was a darkish, smartly dressed young man who carried himself with reserve, dignity, and poise. He became class president, to no one's surprise. Pat and I spoke of how the seminary was split between liberals and conservatives, liberals being those who embraced the modern methods of interpretation and conservatives being those who resisted them. I quickly found myself caught in the murky middle with burning questions having to do with the doctrines I had been given to believe since I was a boy, and which I now began to test against the brightest of my fellow students and even my teachers. One tall former baseball

Mount Tamalpais

player, Don, a senior, blew me away with an answer to a question I had on atonement. I could not beat him in ping-pong either. Bill's room was at the end of the hall. He was a stocky man, a weightlifter. He was a gentle soul too, and a scholar who could read German. He told me about Karl Barth, the theologian who was all the rage here in seminary and all over the country, some of whose volumes he had, though I would have to wait to read them in upper level classes, he said. I liked and trusted Bill and visited with him often. Soon I was in awe of Barth and promised myself that I would master his work some day. Bill said that it was Barth who was responsible for the theological boom that was taking place in Europe and America. Surely Barth was saying something of pivotal importance, the guts of which I should know.

Dr. Arnold Come was the authority on Barthian theology. He had just returned from Germany, where he had studied with Barth himself. A serious man, he lectured with notes that were painstakingly precise. He was teaching a system, consistency and coherence were all-important, and every word counted.

The other theologian was the young, playful new graduate from Princeton Theological Seminary, Dr. Benjamin Reist. Both his lectures and his preaching were articulate, funny, and theatrical, charged with an irrepressible theological swagger. We smiled when he spoke. Someone signed Barth's name on the roll that was being passed around in class. Norm Roddick's impersonation of him was perfect on a Friday entertainment night. His palm stuck to the table, resisting release. When Billy Graham came to speak at the seminary, those two professors sat in the balcony as a sign of rebuff. It was widely known that they disapproved of his visit.

Hard work prevailed in Montgomery Hall. The muffled sound of typewriters emanated from the rooms late into the night. I would listen to the radio at times to the sounds of San Francisco, the jazz, the hit songs like *You Send Me*. Songs have a way of stamping an era with their seal. They shape the soul too. The voices, the lyrics, the rhythm, the melody, and the musical accompaniment all can blend so well that they penetrate, they escalate you to new domains of being and nonbeing. In my room I swayed and drifted with them, hand in hand with the girl of my dreams, from Ferris wheel and boardwalk out to the beach.

The songs I was hearing now had a different gestalt than the mild *Because of You* and *A Kiss to Build a Dream On*, which I had heard on the All India Radio Hit Parade broadcast from what was then Ceylon. These songs now conveyed a dark waterfront ephemerality. Something of a painful transition, perhaps a tipping point long in the making, a smoke gets in your eyes goodbye, was transpiring in the underground of the human soul. On the other hand, *Be Thou My Vision* and *Come Labor On*, two forceful older hymns I learned in my hymnody class, refurbished my reasons for being here in seminary. Pilgrim reader, you should have heard the vigorous sound of our class as we sang them in the stone monastery-style classroom building. I had never heard such powerful singing or such unsentimental and muscular religious music.

If I could only compose this book in musical notes! My symphony is about the still of the night. It starts with the jazz in The Hungry Eye of my imagination. Overtones of the hit songs come and go throughout. The threatening undercurrents of the Bay are realized by the basses and cellos, and the foghorns are heard as deep rumbling undertones. The sadness of Alcatraz, the rocky refuge of Sin and Death, and the ballad of the lonely young man longing for love are conveyed by an extended piano solo using deep, rich chords.

The music is propelled forward by the tensions, each in turn, between the seminary and the city, the East and the West, and the young man and the city's promise of love. A male chorus singing the great hymns in the distance provides a counterpoint both to the flutes and gongs and movie songs of India and the Far East and to the desperate, abstract sounds of the city's night secrets. "High King of heaven, my victory won" and the other lines of the hymns, not yet phrased in contemporary and gender-inclusive language, come out of the hills softly in the north wind and float mellifluously on the water like the lanterns of peace, swelling into a crescendo as they approach the city's harbor. The Golden Gate Bridge, the arc of opportunity, reconciliation, and welcome, is rendered by the soaring lyrics of a soprano with a lucid, lambent voice pouring down like the full moon upon the big city, the waters, and Marin county, Tamalpais looming, on the north side.

Down the other end of the hallway from where Bill's room was I would hear someone playing Rachmaninoff's *Rhapsody on a Theme of Paganini* on his stereo, and I also remember hearing the old American folk song *Shenandoah* sung by Norman Luboff-style singers. Both pieces made me stand at the door of my room. The melancholy folk song carried me deep into the American heartland and back and away vaguely into the civil war. A cast on my arm, I was bleeding for the smiling valley and the rolling river far, far away across the wide Missouri.

3

Sacred Ground

*Buber's simple thoughts stream from
the page into the understanding*

IT WAS A MONSOON of spiritual and intellectual ferment. My traditional faith, nurtured in a praying and pious Indian Christian home in which I was the son and grandson of pastors, would not do well in a seminary culture given to open dialogue and driven by the quest for learning. The pictures on the walls of our home in Ferozepore, the strong arms of the Good Shepherd reaching over the cliff's edge to save the lamb, the tearful Christ with the crown of thorns knocking on the door, Christ in Gethsemane, were incongruous with the books and the music in my room. John Paul Sartre's play *No Exit*, produced by the student theater group, further expanded my horizons and told me I was a self very much in the making.

In this creative atmosphere of crosscurrents the big question insinuated itself upon me like Leviathan suddenly appearing beside the ship. I was reading it in books. It was written in the walls of modernity and carried on the winds of the times, even printed in the fire of the human chest and the fog of theology. It was the question of the magi, as I was to learn later, in W.B. Yeats' poem of 1914: Unconvinced by Calvary, the pale unsatisfied ones probe the uncontrollable mystery on the bestial floor. It was the quest of *The Other Wise Man* in Henry Van Dyke's classic story. Artaban misses his meeting in Borsippa with the magi of scripture because he stops in the dark grove of date palms in Babylon to heal a dying Hebrew. The story has the hero come up empty in his stated search for the One whose star he had seen in Persia, but there is yet the deeper hunger for the true meaning of his long journey. This hidden and obscure troubledness brings him over the years to wounded beings who stand in need of healing, protection, and freedom.

In particular it was the simple little paperback *I and Thou* by the theologian Martin Buber that left me with a not yet recognized quarrel with the systematic theology I was studying. It had just been published in English and was already beginning to cause ripples in American thought. Buber had no grand system to promulgate or protect. His simple thoughts streamed from the page into the understanding and the cells of the body, no need to cast about for proof.

The book focuses on the relationship signified by the words I and Thou, which when spoken engage the whole being, not just the intellect or emotion. What is the I without the Thou? Just an isolated, desolate reed shaken by the wind. Its voice is never heard. It is unvisited, vacant, autistic. But the I and its Thou in their interaction experience integrity, fullness, and power as living beings. Their voices project irresistibly to the four corners of the café. They are the cynosure of all eyes and ears.

I and Thou are also contrasted by Buber with I and It. The I and It relationship is not spoken with the whole being. Buber gives the example of a tree. It is beautiful, you are lost in its warm autumn glow, and your response is sensuous and spontaneous and whole. Your I and Thou relation with the tree is direct and immediate. The tree is a subject, a living being speaking to you in its own language of colors and lines. But this very Thou, Buber warns, must become an object and lose its property of being a subject. Your relation to it will inevitably become an I-It relation.

You leave that place near the stone bridge, now enchanted, and walk down the trail beside the river, thinking back about the tree. The memory lingers with its yellow dust. You think, How the fallen leaves made such a perfect circle beneath the tree. You remember, Did not my heart burn within me as I stood beside that tree? Did not that place become a sacred ground, and the tree a burning bush that was not consumed? You muse, How every living being has a body, an age, a spring, an autumn. And as you walk between the river and the carpet of wildflowers you wonder, How life is even more beautiful and precious in its vulnerability and evanescence.

But now you have drifted into your head in relation to that tree. Though your thoughts still glow in its luminous splendor, the tree is now a mere object in those thoughts. Furthermore, the world is expanding to be larger than that single tree. New entities appear that become for you a Thou. A wooden footbridge crossing the river comes into view and occupies the mind.

Even at that young age I could tell that Buber's work constituted a momentous breakthrough in the area of religion. I and Thou contained a treasure chest of implications which I could at most intuit then. For one thing, I took from it what was still a crude understanding of Truth in the big, capitalized sense as a sort of guide. Our ideas are True in the big sense insofar as they are transparent of their I and Thou ground of being. To the extent that they lose contact with ground control, they lose their Truth. Our theology classes in seminary were so academic, straying so far down the street from their reason for being, that they often left us cold, unsatisfied, uncertain as to their Truth.

Buber was raised in a home in which the primary relationship, namely the I and Thou, between his mother and father was broken. In his autobiographical writings he says that his nanny's words about his mother, "No, she will never come back," cleaved to his heart. He must have pondered the gendered nature of I and Thou, having read almost certainly the pioneering study of Ludwig Feuerbach on that subject.

It is possible that he even distanced himself unconsciously from I and Thou. He writes of the silence of the workers when he delivered lectures on religion in the folk-school. The silence became painfully clear by the third evening. One worker came and explained that they were not allowed to speak, and would Professor Buber be willing to meet with them the next evening at a different venue? He did go to the agreed place, and an older person challenged him about God. Suddenly the atmosphere was strained, and Buber's arguments backed the man into a corner.

Again there was silence. In that second silence Buber came to confront the tragic primal fact. He had presented in his lectures merely the I-It God of the philosophers, depriving the workers of the Eternal Thou. In particular, he had not been truly present as Thou for this man. His ego had gotten the better of him, and now it was late in the day.

4

Market Street

If you're young, take a chance if you love her

Buber regretted his comportment toward the workers, having left them not with the Eternal Thou, but with the philosophers' God of the intellect. In 1933 after he was dismissed from the university, he continued to be present in Germany for his people instead of leaving for Palestine. In the face of the boycott, the deprivation of civil service jobs, the Reich Citizenship Law, and the lengthening shadows of harassment and horror, he continued to counsel and console.

Though I could not connect the dots all around and beyond the sky, I intuited the singular truth of Buber's message. I possessed it, I grew into it as I had grown into my father's New York City suits as a teenager. It was not clear to me how exactly the Eternal Thou, God, fit into the I and Thou scheme of things. This nagged at me. The best I could do was to say that particular I and Thou relationships are in some sense perhaps sacred ground, and that a particular Thou is related in some murky sense to the Eternal Thou. The God question was turning out to be the big and momentous question quite early in my life.

Did I see the face of the Eternal Thou in the face of Paul and Mary Bodine? A short and stocky freshman, soft-spoken but articulate, Paul was carrying a full academic load. He did not have a full scholarship as I did. He delivered newspapers on the narrow streets winding up and down the hills in the foggy mornings, and he came to class tired, not having read his assignments. His background was conservative too, and we talked when we could. Paul and Mary took the trouble to have me over for dinner in their small rented house on one of the hills.

My visit was an intimate look into their life. She was pale and very pretty, with a round face. Hugely pregnant too, and shy, blushing easily. We spoke of her Salvation Army background and their courtship, and we noted that she wore no lipstick. It is sad that we lost touch so soon as the academic years progressed, as often students do. I have treasured them like old photographs in my heart for a long, long time. Were they reflections in a metaphysical pond of the Eternal Thou? This question, in truth, was not yet fully formed in my mind, but waiting for its time, like a road that one has seen but not yet had a reason to travel.

I spoke of I and Thou with an Arab student I met at the International House in Berkeley. It was lonely at the seminary on holidays. Most of the single students went home. I had taken the bus to Berkeley to look for someone to be with, but it was just as empty on that campus. The coffee shop was open, and I ordered a milkshake. The Arab student and his young blue-eyed female companion prepared it for me, giggling and flirting.

The young man did come and sit with me at a booth, probably at my invitation. He was a graduate student in economics and spoke of how he would apply his studies to the situation in his country. He smiled dismissively when I explained my own interest in theology and the new book by the Jewish theologian Martin Buber. To introduce the Eternal Thou into the universe of discourse, however, felt more labored than logical. He looked over his shoulder to his companion. Serious purpose and resolve were carved in the dark ancient lines of his face, but he was distracted now, full of fire and mischief, his eyes giddy with delight and desire. His obsession with the young woman reigned supreme over our dialogue, which ended shortly. Was I in encounter with the Eternal Thou in some important sense, in the person of both the man across the table and perhaps the woman behind the counter?

A small but quite memorable thing happened on my first Thanksgiving Day. Interesting how such seemingly insignificant moments become part of the architecture of our minds. I was grateful to be invited by the student body treasurer and his wife Alice for dinner that day. I was directed to sit next to Alice's sister, who appeared in my sky like a dazzling comet with a trailing flare. That was when a spry, preppy, flamboyant woman sat next to a dimwit who was pulled to her by his roots. Which fork do I use anyway? Do I eat the salad first? Was I being invited to be her boyfriend?

The Meaning of These Days

That couldn't be! If only I was capable of pursuit. I hated my oversized dull brown suit, which made me look only skinnier and browner against this celestial luminary.

Was this house of fire and fog in some sense sacred ground?

It turned out that I could drown the pain, if only temporarily, of the thorn of anxiety both of my discomfiture in intimate situations like this and of something like individualized existence itself. That the anomie was not a temporary condition but a permanent inhabitant of this clay vessel was sinking in as a foregone conclusion. I began taking the Greyhound bus into San Francisco. The Hungry Eye, known for its jazz, was too far away from the bus depot. It was on or just off Market Street that I saw *The Young Lions* and *Love Is a Many-Splendored Thing* and ate Mars Bars in grand cinemas and submerged myself in dark adult amusement arcades and burlesque shows of comedy acts and dance routines harking back to vaudeville. On the screen I saw women in bathing suits frolicking, shaking supposedly to the swing music of small combos and big bands. It was amusing, however, how the music of Benny Goodman, Artie Shaw, and the Dorsey brothers was tacked on so out of sync. While the music changed, the reel continued in dead silence.

Most shops were closed on holidays. My face went by in the windows up and down the lonely boulevard. The one place always open day and night was the bus depot cafe. There I sat and watched the "Anchors Away" navy men in uniform milling about waiting for their buses. I played Frank Sinatra on the juke box, "If you're young, take a chance if you love her. Tell her you love her, tell her you love her." The song was an abyss of dread for young inept lovers who craved tenderness but were afraid to risk themselves enough to say, Could you put up with me forever? And their ship was waiting in the harbor.

For me there was no Thou but for the waitress. At the counter alone with its apple pie, coffee, and cigarettes, the I was vagrant and impotent. It was voiceless except to ask for the remaining piece of pie or a refill. In the asking, however, its voice was heard and for a fleeting moment the cup brimmed over. And the song continued, becoming urgent, "Tell her now before it's too late. And before she belongs to another. . .." By now the young wilted I was a prisoner in Alcatraz looking into the waters of futility. It was said that no one has escaped by swimming across from the prison island to the mainland, the undercurrents being so powerful.

Market Street

In the middle of the night there were few passengers. The dark vinyl seats soaked up whatever light there was. The hit songs played in my head as the bus moved across Golden Gate Bridge and through the sleeping towns. The driver called out their names as we came to them, Sausalito, Mill Valley, Larkspur. The street lamps glowered down in the fog as a passenger got off the bus and walked away. The classy Foster and Kleiser and other billboards drew the eye on the freeway as we passed them. The freeways were brand new then. Everyone was talking about how one could drive forever without coming to a light. This luxury blinded us all. No one saw how these roadways would proliferate. No one understood their true meaning in terms of their political provenance or their human and nonhuman consequences.

When we came to San Anselmo the driver glanced at me in his mirror.

5

Yosemite Valley

I sat down by the river and read

I WAS SPLIT INTO two Kierkegaardian halves, intellect and existence. On the intellectual level I was applying myself well, asking good questions in class, impressing my teachers and classmates with my love of learning, getting As in my theology classes though doing only fair in Hebrew and Greek, church history, and the psychology of religion. I was truly eager for this new knowledge and the new perspective and promise to which it would surely lead. It was the early dawn of my theological awakening, and I was impatient to see what the new day would bring. I even bought a new book by a Princeton theologian to read during the summer months when I would be working at Yosemite National Park. Sin and Death were present too in the form of Pride and Wrath. I became arrogant in the imagination of my heart, quarrelsome even with some of my teachers.

On the existential level, the level on which we live, move, and have our being, I was carried away by the undercurrents of the Bay Area waters. I knew when the buses came and went, and I braved the fog, cold winds, and damp air to lose myself in the neon of Market Street. I would not be held prisoner to a traditional piety that was plagued by misgivings, and whose walls were disintegrating against the tsunami force of life itself and the sheer size of the world. This secret manifesto was issued quite unconsciously by the way I was trying to forge my survival as my own bewildered self in this new situation whose dangers and mysteries I did not know.

What I craved was carnal knowledge. Why could not I breach the confines of this theological hill, find my way to The Hungry Eye, listen to *Bye*

Yosemite Valley

Bye, Blackbird, and quiver to the tapping of the cymbals, the hollow echoes of the base, and the weeping of the saxophone? Who sat at those tables? Was there a counter? Was there dancing, a crooner? Would I be shown to a seat, and would I cast a long shadow? How much would it cost? Let Sin and Death, now as Lust and its reverberations of Wrath, prowl. The mind was crazy with imagination and desire. I would taste of the salt winds of freedom. I would comb the waterfront for all the dark vacant corners where women and men came to watch the sea.

If there was a Golden Gate Bridge between the two levels, it was Martin Buber, who knew the power of the Bay Area undercurrents over an empty vessel. And I knew in turn that any theology presenting itself for my assent must first pass the muster of I and Thou. The Buddhist theologian Takeuchi Yoshinori calls the similar bridge between the hither shore and the yonder shore the bridge of transcendence. One can cross over in either direction both on the Takeuchi Bridge and on the Golden Gate Bridge between intellect and existence.

My first summer in America was spent working for the Curry Company in Yosemite Valley and helping out with the National Parks Ministry. The seminary had arranged for this, and I had the chance to work with young adults from all over the country. One young woman from Mississippi had a relationship with a Lebanese cook. I looked at that heavyweight man with the chef's white uniform and hat with a wave of jealousy. I was well aware of being drawn to her myself. Aside from her classical face, there was something withdrawn and unreachable about her. This was something inherent in her, I suspected, not a front she put on to keep others at arm's length.

I assisted with Sunday morning worship services held outdoors next to Yosemite Falls close to the Lodge. The Reverend Glass was park chaplain and pastor of the small wooden church where evening services were held. The real inspiration for all who came to Yosemite, however, were the monumental vertical cliffs and the waterfalls that made us lift up our eyes, Half Dome and El Capitan too, the Merced River winding through the valley, the flowers in the meadow, the fresh smell of the pines, the deer and the bear, the singing of *Apple Blossom Time* at the campfires and singalongs, the back country hiking, the serendipity of meeting people from all over the world, the pitch blackness of the night.

The new theology book I had bought was George S. Hendry's *The Gospel of the Incarnation*. Between the afternoon and the evening shifts I would go to the river and sit among the tall grasses to read. Page by page I devoured the wisdom of this theologian, trusting him more and more as I read. All year long I had studied and written papers on the history of Christian dogma and how the theologians are at pains to make it come alive today. But except perhaps for Oscar Cullman's thesis that cyclical time was a Greek concept and linear time was what was avowed by the early Christian texts, their pages were arduous and dull, still freighted with medieval metaphysics. They had not disabused me of the fundamentalist doctrines and the pictures on the wall of my formative years in India. I was a passionate but norm-less young man at one of the most important crossroads of my spiritual life, and I was floundering on what exactly to be passionate about. Here came Hendry with guidance as fresh as this river from the high country snows.

Hendry's approach was similar to Buber's. Having disentangled itself from traditional doctrines and systems, it appealed now to relational existence as the final arbiter of Truth in the big theological sense. Do not think of the atonement as transfixed in one moment of time. Do not view the traditional Christian doctrines through windows stained with manufactured philosophies and theologies you cannot understand. Imagine them, rather, in the contours and colors of the natural world unfolding in the table fellowship and the healing and reconciling ministry of Jesus, which for Hendry was the true meaning of the incarnation and the key to the meaning of Christian faith itself.

Sitting by the Merced River that summer I was thus encouraged to rethink my religion in an organic, relational language. I began to understand Jesus in terms of his I and Thou encounter with other persons, his being fully present for them in a way that Buber himself had not been for the German factory workers, and in terms of his solidarity with the blind, the deaf, the lame, the mentally ill, the unloved. A person for other persons, said Hendry, is what the scripture means when it says that Jesus took upon himself the sin and sickness of others. The suffering servant passage was quoted by Matthew in Chapter 8 not in connection with a single moment in time, Jesus' death, but to apply to his healing ministry. It was this latter that was said to fulfill what was spoken by the prophet Isaiah, namely that the suffering servant took our infirmities and bore our diseases.

Hendry's explanations came like a flash of lightning. They illuminated the spiritual landscape and showed me the foothold I needed in my early rummaging for meaning and truth. The different theories I had studied of the atonement had only clouded my mind and left me with questions. Hendry's incarnational theology not only anticipated what has only recently come into fairly wide acceptance, but it made eminent human sense when I sorely needed my religion to make sense. That sense now became as luminous as the color of wild flowers blowing in the summer wind, and as immediate as looking up to see tourists float down the river on their rafts.

6

Tioga Pass

My Barth volumes went missing on the way to Tuolumne Meadows

All my belongings fit into two cardboard boxes, which I checked on to the bus as I headed for Yosemite the next summer. The Agape Fellowship was a two-year scholarship for Asian students, and the seminary directed me to go and finish my BA degree before going on to my senior year. I had applied to various colleges but they would not accept my credits from India. What was I to do? I had nowhere to go that fall. I trusted that a door would open somehow, but the seriousness of my quandary would sink deeper and deeper as the summer progressed.

Furthermore, it was probably in Merced, where I think I changed buses, that my heavier box containing my theology books, including several volumes of Karl Barth's *Church Dogmatics*, went missing. I had spent my precious little scholarship money to buy them. I filled out the paperwork when I got to Yosemite, but nothing came of it.

At Yosemite the Curry Company assigned me to work not down in the valley this time but in the back country, up at Tuolumne Meadows at around 8,000 feet. I hitchhiked up to Tioga Pass from the valley in the back of a pick-up truck. My boss was Mike Adams, who I learned later was the son of the famous Yosemite photographer Ansel Adams. He was a breezy, fun kind of person to work for. A jet pilot in the Air Force Reserve, he promised he would buzz our camp while on a practice mission. I was in the kitchen washing dishes when he flew right over. I had missed it.

Tioga Pass

Again young women and men from all over were my colleagues at Tuolumne Lodge, the blond, blue-eyed beaming Sweetheart of Sigma Chi at the University of California at Berkeley, two young women from Vassar, a dark-haired brother and sister pair from La Jolla, and many others. Many of these names and terms were new to me then. We did kitchen work, cleaned tents, changed bed sheets, served meals. An uncouth, swashbuckling young man with glasses and cigarettes had a pick-up truck, and he and I took the garbage to the dump early every morning. The bears would be waiting, some up in the trees, and we were both anxious to be done.

The care of the horses and the dusty stables was left to the cowboys and cowgirls, seasoned permanent employees. I stole looks at one of them, a tall attractive taciturn woman with boots and hat and sculpted features, as if she was out of a Zane Grey novel or a Gary Cooper movie. She may well have been already attached with another man; I never came to know. She looked stately on a horse, staunch against the mountain sky.

To help with the Sunday morning services and the campfire singalongs I went from tent to tent distributing fliers in the public campgrounds close to the Lodge. The Reverend Woodruff, who had replaced the Reverend Glass as park chaplain, supervised my volunteer work. Who had I to turn to but to him about my quandary regarding what I should or could do in the fall? Out of concern for me he wrote and inquired about the possibility of my admission into Chapman College, his own alma mater, a Disciples of Christ college in southern California. To my great relief Chapman admitted me with two years' worth of credit for the academic work I had done in India.

A door of opportunity had suddenly swung wide open. Though those were kinder days, I moved through dense clouds of anxiety at Tioga Pass. I was young, alone, in a foreign land, and on the road to anywhere. I shudder to think what might have happened had the Reverend Woodruff not been there for me. To this day I remain grateful to that caring man, a pastor who helped open for me the door to America, the land of the Shenandoah and its smiling valley and rolling river. I learned early that a pastor's job is to find a way across the wide Missouri. The way to yonder shore is just what Takeuchi calls the bridge of transcendence.

In my spiritual life the religion of the past continued to glance apprehensively at the theological ideas that would guide my future. I was equipped now with words like existential and historicity and such primal and radical information that it was as if I possessed a secret neo-orthodox crypt granted only to initiates at the San Anselmo seminary to decode. But this knowledge still coexisted in my soul with the pictures on the wall and the mantelpiece in my aunt's home in Ferozepore.

No, Pilgrim, my new learning did not overrule Jesus in Gethsemane, Jesus reaching over the cliff for the lamb caught in the bramble bush, the tearful Jesus with crown of thorns knocking on the massive door of the human heart, the aureate face of Jesus at twelve in a shining robe, the Bible verses and the Gospel songs, the preaching and singing voices of the Bible-carrying missionaries up in Landour, the koinonia and charisma in the ashram of E. Stanley Jones, my grandfather's unending prayers at Christmas, with the large family sitting on beds and chairs and wicker stools and arrived on famous trains from Lahore and the northwest frontier, the land of the Pathans, and from the ancient cities of Amritsar and Delhi. At those prayers I confess to peeping at times.

That family exists no more. It grew apart, like families do, as the older generation died and the new generation adapted to the circumstances and pressures of the twentieth century. Those sounds and images, however, continued to anchor, guard, and confine my thinking. The women at Tuolumne saw me as different. They went to other men or to no men at all. That they did this left me, I admit, slowly burning inside, a condition I would have to learn to live with. But they had their own lives to live, why should they bother with my tug of war interiority? It was not that I was brown and spoke with an accent. I was myself detached and insecure and afraid. I used my angular kind of religiousness to serve my instincts and keep me apart. I covered up my hungers well.

The days at Tuolumne Meadows grew short. Dragonflies, tiny helicopters, flew up and down the stream cascading down the gently sloping but muscular mountainside. Come, Pilgrim, we will go and sit among the boulders and shrubs, above the Lodge where the ranger presents at the campfire weekly and they sing *Amazing Grace* and *Let Me Call You Sweetheart*. Let us sit and watch the inexhaustible energy of the water, listen to the scolding of the blue-jays, and brood upon the sermons of the season.

And I can take you, Pilgrim, further upstream to more pools of unruly waters with swirling twigs and petals and bark and wings and mottled leaves and vestiges of the same, transient beings making their way to the sea. They move and are free and we are glad for them. They have had their high mountain summer in the sun, in the rain, in the cold wind. They became bold in the presence of their enemies, steadfast against the gates of hell, intelligent in temptation. They were delicate in love, and they shone brightly in their day, staying the assault of the darkness. Where then is your sting, O death? Where your victory, O grave? Let them seek out their sea, or their new soil, in a softer place where the sun sets, far below Tioga Pass. We can go to the quiet waters too, the still waters, the softly flowing dreamy and bright waters further downstream, near where the meadows begin, across the winding blue highway.

7

The Scream

*Niebuhr cast his net far and wide
over human experience*

I first saw Ruth, as I recall, in the cafeteria line. She stood tall and was classically pretty. Her face was fair and soft and uncluttered, pale at times. She smiled, laughed, and giggled easily with her friends. I saw a man paying attention to her. They talked often, and I grew jealous. Much later there was another man. I do not remember actually talking to her in the first few weeks, but my infatuation already knew no bounds.

The old town atmosphere of Orange, Chapman College, and the orange groves next to the new dorms with no fence between them felt like I wouldn't mind being here forever. It felt summery and settled compared to the jagged emotions of New Delhi and St. Stephens, the cool foggy green of Mt. Tamalpais, the blue winds and scary currents of the Bay Area waters, the saturated clouds of unknowing at Tioga Pass. The only problem was Ruth.

A relaxed down-home camaraderie and friendship prevailed among the students and professors. Carroll Cotton, the men's dorm supervisor, beat me easily in ping-pong, but he let me watch *The Streets of Laredo* again in his suite. Mike, a classmate, liked to talk about politics, and he became a good friend. My vociferous suite mate kept me posted on what he knew about Ruth. He darted around in his green MG, in which I myself was an occasional passenger. What an uncaged sort of guy, I thought, nothing bothers him. He always has something to say and is never at a loss for words. He goes where he pleases, and the MG was made just for him. He is friends with everyone and mad about no one.

A congenial space seemed to open up in which I could wander and muse. There was less pressure in Orange than there had been at St. Stephens. I lived in the dorms, I did not have to be part of an elite, and I went to the movies with other foreign students. I started working as a part-time youth assistant under the Reverend Green, who was the associate pastor at the First Presbyterian Church close by.

Dr. Bert C. Williams was my venerable philosophy teacher at the college, a kind and gray Boston humanist with thick glasses and a mustache. He did not hesitate to admit that he embraced the humanist philosophy of Edgar Sheffield Brightman, whose coherence-based argument for the existence of God we had to read. A lean figure with pointed features, Dr. Williams would huddle over the text on the table to explicate the material quite literalistically, exactly the way he wanted us to reproduce it on a test.

Edward Munch's *The Scream* was one of the works of art pictured in black and white on the frontispiece of our history of philosophy text by W. T. Jones. I looked at it and heard the scream every time I opened the big book. The existentialistic readings in San Anselmo and my exposure to *No Exit* had prepared me well for a philosophy major, though sitting in class I could sense that a marriage between theology and philosophy might quickly become problematic.

I grew to recognize *The Scream* as an iconic image of modernity. The dark secrets of existence, heretofore told only in whispers, could now be shouted on bridges, told in bazaars, wept out loudly in railway junctions. Clandestine shames will find ears, suppressed stories will find a voice. Such was the promise of the times. Existence before essence, asseverated Sartre as existentialism's manifesto. For better or worse we are thrown into an alienated, ambiguous, and deracinated world to make our own way, secure our own life, create our own meaning, learn from our own mistakes, find our own love. There is no metaphysical template against which to measure, no *a priori* norm to be a lamp to our feet and a light for our path, no plan laid before the foundation of the world for the fullness of our days.

This attitude of mind, however, was already setting me on a collision course with the mainstream of Western philosophy. I admit I was impressed by existentialism's unyielding gaze into the cavernous depths of absurdity, angst, authenticity, nothingness, and freedom. Furthermore, had not theology found in existentialism a new language fertile for its own explorations of the subterranean recesses of the human soul? Had it not found a perch from which to critique the spiritually bankrupt culture of Babylon? I still note with interest the frequency with which the word existential is used nowadays with a somewhat different, more literal and political meaning, even in broadcast journalism.

Day by day, week by week in Dr. Williams' class, however, I was being drenched in philosophies of reason, from Plato to Wittgenstein, with their interest not in the I and Thou of critical presence or in the alienations and anxieties of human subjectivity at all, but in logic, clarity of thought, and the foundations of knowledge. The big question percolating now in my soul had to do with the dissonance between these two alien frames of reference. It was as if two different languages with two different universes, each with its own firmament of suns and moons and stars, were in combat. I am not describing again the tension between intellect and existence, alluded to in a previous chapter, but rather the potentially rocky intellectual relationship between philosophy and theology. But Pilgrim, we will voyage together in this book to both universes and learn both languages.

We start by going back to a point in time one hundred years or so before I arrived in Orange. We flash back for a quick moment to the old standoff between Kierkegaard and Bishop Mynster in Denmark. Even though theirs was not a clash between philosophy as such and theology, it is a good example of how a theologian can question longstanding tradition and erudition, and how she or he may detect the will to power, self-contentment, and self-deception operative in them.

Kierkegaard was the father of existentialism and Bishop Mynster the cultivated, shrewd, refined establishment Brahmin of Christendom who believed that the church should be kept secure and content by the state. Kierkegaard denounced Bishop Mynster publicly in the press, saying, You are mad with all the worldly pleasures and advantages of your position. You accept not one iota of Christianity's teachings about renunciation and dying to oneself and being unhappy in this life. You deem the king and the priests and the wellborn infinitely more important than the beggar and the commoner.

My sympathies were very much with Kierkegaard. I still find reading his writings to be like being baptized at 8000 feet in Tenaya Lake, joltingly alarming and refreshing. His vehement attack on Christian hypocrisy, his expressions of solidarity with the beggar and the commoner, and his bald and piercing portrayal of the sickness of human interiority represent to me the best of the existentialist theology I had learned in San Anselmo. But how was I when I was young to weigh Kierkegaard and his theology of existence against the bishops and archbishops of the rationalistic philosophical establishment of the West? Furthermore, was not Kierkegaard on the verge of madness? Was it not just his unbearable manic-depressive condition that catapulted him into his faith?

The vague sense of fragmentation growing within me was validated by a paperback I bought that first year in Orange. Morton White's *Social Thought in America* was about important intellectuals in the early part of the twentieth century in America. Chief among them was John Dewey, who helped develop pragmatism, the philosophy of the use of intelligence in human affairs. I bought that book mainly because the brand new edition contained an epilogue which included a critique of Reinhold Niebuhr, and I held my breath as White's considerable philosophical firepower let loose on the theologian. It was a personal thing with me because of my own investment in theology and because my father had often spoken admiringly of Niebuhr as a stimulating and erudite teacher with whom he had had seminars.

What was shaping up for me was a major heavyweight battle between a gifted and courageous existentialist theologian and an important Western philosopher, John Dewey, represented now by White. It was Niebuhr who had launched his critique of Dewey's alleged naive optimism about the application of intelligence to human affairs. Niebuhr had flung his net far and wide over human experience to come up with gems about how and why it was inevitable that Dewey's admittedly humane project would stall. Sin is the serpent spoiler in the garden of reason, warned Niebuhr, in the tradition of Paul, Augustine, and Kierkegaard, and he expounded at length about the depth of greed, vested interests, hubris, lust, the will to power, and all manner of corporate egoism sabotaging the liberal hopes of thinkers like Dewey. Neibuhr insisted that the plans we form, the policies we put in place, must take these surd, untidy, unsettling facts into account.

White, however, defended Dewey and launched his own polemic against Niebuhr. Among other things, Niebuhr appeals to authority. It is the Pauline doctrine of original sin that lies behind his talk about the inevitability of sin. His talk at once about the inevitability of sin and human responsibility for sin is inconsistent. He offers no alternative to the use of our intelligence to make our way forward in the world. White's diatribe went on and on.

The Meaning of These Days

Even at my young age I could see the two different languages and their two distinct universes at work. White was squirmy about the whole idea of sin, let alone the inevitability of sin, as if it was a harking back to some voodoo age of platitudinous gibberish. Even though he said that he agreed with Niebuhr politically, he inveighed against admitting Niebuhr into the halls of philosophical respectability. Brute, primal, and often obscure complexity was a reality belonging to a murky alien universe whose language he could not countenance in modern civilized discourse. Resolved to reduce public dialogue to its lowest, most logical and linear denominator, he was a good example of what the great nineteenth century theologian Friedrich Schleiermacher called a cultured despiser of religion.

For my part, I was instinctively on the side of Niebuhr, just as I had been on the side of Kierkegaard in his clash with Bishop Mynster. Not only could I understand the existential language of religion but it seemed to fit me like an old shoe. Sin and Death were still at my heels, and I knew them well. They darkened the counsel of my mind and foiled my best and brightest intentions. I knew that Niebuhr was hardly appealing to authority in his talk about sin, but rather to the tragic in human history. Yet I was unable to sift through the logical wheat and chaff to defend Niebuhr adequately. I let the unrest in my mind and soul lie for the time being. I was clearly not yet ready to resolve it, and I knew that I would return to it when the time was right.

Furthermore I had to attend to my own existence on the ground. Willful as it was, this was such an expansive time to be alive. The orange groves cast their old world glow and fragrance upon the new inventions. The horizon was receding on a daily basis. Los Angeles and Hollywood were just to the north, and they were calling. The beaches were just to the west, and they too were calling. Friday was a good movie impatient to be reached. Saturday was a beach, a surfboard, and the waves of the sea.

8

Los Angeles
In the wee small hours of the morning

I KEPT A SAFE distance from Ruth. There were other men, whose eyes I avoided. Did she know how I felt? Did she feel the same way about me? Her feminine voice and the stately way she held her head aloft filled my dreams, and every day in the quad, the cafeteria, and the classroom hallways I was demure and concealed my shyness.

Except for my ineptitude in love and the perpetual stinging sensation inside, I was happy in southern California. Hollywood, the beaches, the hit songs on the radio, and the palm tree avenues of Los Angeles promised light ocean breezes, dreamy musical rendezvous, soft summer nights, and dancing under the stars. Disneyland had the big Benny Goodman band playing under a large tent canopy, and I danced with a dark-haired brown-eyed young woman, who gave me her phone number.

I had learned how to drive in a flashy red convertible 1957 Thunderbird with automatic transmission. It belonged to a member of our young adult group at First Presbyterian, Paul, who was the son of a local businessman. He was mild-mannered, tall and freckle-faced, with a generous smile; the color of his car was just a shade darker than his hair. Driving his car to Newport Beach and Corona Del Mar with the top down and parallel parking it on a crowded street on a Saturday intoxicated me with breezy joy.

My own first car was a shapely old blue convertible stick-shift Ford which lacked power going uphill, but the radio blared out the new hits: *Soldier Boy, Do You Wanna Dance, A Summer Place*. Joanie Sommers' *One Boy* was my favorite. Her lilting voice was buoyant and wafting like the waves of the sea. She was the one who later did the jingle *Now It's Pepsi for Those Who Think Young*. Some of us foreign students went to see Hitchcock's *Psycho* in Fullerton. The movie and its screaming music during the shower scene were to be talked about forever after.

The Santa Ana Freeway was only three or four years old then, and the last miles to Laguna Beach were still a lovely rural drive through the hills of native shrubs and grass. I remember a country store and fruit stands along the way, and the advening waves were in the air.

The sleek blue convertible with the top down was even sleeker on the Pacific Coast Highway and on immaculate Sunset Boulevard among the gated gardens and homes of the movie stars. I had flashbacks of the dead body in the pool in *Sunset Boulevard*. I was the intrepid Gary Cooper in *High Noon*, and the song in my heart was *Do Not Forsake Me, O My Darling*. I was Marlon Brando, the illiterate peasant who stood up and drawled "Zapata" when the official asked who had spoken and what his name was. I was the brooding, tragic Montgomery Clift pining for Elizabeth Taylor in *A Place in the Sun*.

But more than Burt Lancaster's famous scene with Deborah Kerr on the beach, more than the Montgomery Clift or the Frank Sinatra character, it was Sinatra singing the prelude *From Here to Eternity* in the movie of that name that set me adrift on the dark waters of the imagination. Love is fugitive, like the ebb and flow of the sea. It springs up and gives, and then it takes away.

Downtown Los Angeles had its share of B-movie theaters, sleaze bars, old navy and army clothes outlets, cafeterias, and ten cent stores. The grander cinemas and expensive restaurants were on Sunset and Hollywood Boulevards in Hollywood. "Girls Girls Girls" was the flashing neon sign at venues where you could pay money to dance or sit with the hostess of your choice. At one place you climbed up the stairs, bought tickets for your minutes, and found your spot with the decent and indecent, rich and poor, American and foreign, young and wrinkled, all lonely men standing or sitting opposite the women waiting to be asked.

In those days there was a live band playing standards like *Blue Moon* and *It's Only a Paper Moon*, but this was all soon to change to the broadcasting of recordings in the same jazz tradition: Peggy Lee's *Fever*, Sinatra's *All the Way*, and other songs he did in collaboration with Nelson Riddle and his orchestra. Teamed up with Riddle, Sinatra was becoming bigger than ever.

Los Angeles

To the hostess's chagrin, I asked her to abide strictly by the ten minutes I had. The richer men got the lion's share of the time with the prettiest women, but this did not matter much to me. The couples shimmying and swinging and swaying to the music and the glow of the paper moon filled my aching, aching heart. The big anonymous city with its skyscrapers and night lights and amusements and movies and music helped keep me sane and tided me over the worst hours.

I was hermaphroditic, half seminary and half college, half Indian and half American, half religious and half worldly, half running away from and half craving for closeness with Ruth. I seemed to be on the fringe of everything there was.

One woman at the dance club actually reminded me of Ruth. She too was tall, with a touch of elegance and a pale shapely countenance. Ruth stood out in the crowd. Once in the cafeteria line I saw her standing quietly and looking straight ahead like a statue, as if she knew that she was the center of gravity. It was astounding, like California slipping into the sea, that my philosophy studies were going as well as they were.

Clueless as to what to do, but knowing that I had to do something, I had taken a chance. I went to her in the library and asked her if I could talk to her. We went outside and sat on the grass, and I did something I will never, never do again. I actually told her my feelings prematurely. She said that she had a serious relationship with her boyfriend going to college elsewhere. Nervous beyond your imagination, I ended the conversation there and then. I was relieved that I had gotten the matter off my chest. Finished and done with.

Actually it worsened the situation. The romantic tension between us seemed no longer something suppressed, but an outward and obvious fact.

Now as I watched this woman who resembled Ruth, the other women standing across from me, and the couples lost in each other on the dance floor, and as I heard the strains of *Willow Weep for Me*, it was easy to forget my love troubles. For these few hours I too was lost in the preternatural frenzy of ants finding sugar, especially on a holiday with its special party commotion and decorations and skimpy costumes the women wore, and I found solace in the precious few minutes of face to face, I and Thou conversation I could afford with the other. On New Year's Eve I was not alone. On Christmas evening I had somewhere to go. On Independence Day I had something to look forward to.

The Meaning of These Days

You know she wants you somewhere deep down. She wants to come to know you better, but you do not give her the chance. You are shy, and you await the fullness of time. Here in this club you pay your money and there is little risk. You pay your money and you can dance cheek to cheek even with the pretty one, if she agrees to dance with you for a paltry ten minutes, strictly kept. You pay your money and now you stand out from the other men. Now the world can watch you float, glide on the floor and see what you really know, how cool, suave you really are, what poise you have. You are vulnerable, yes, but no one sees that now. The evening has been framed by *Stormy Weather* or the wail of a saxophone. Behind your streetcar of desire is the steam engine known as love, invisible in the night. No one knows, except a Sinatra song, the magnitude, the futile melancholy of your isolation. In the wee small hours of the morning, that's when you miss her most of all.

9

Mount Baldy

The courage to be in the face of nonbeing

I WAS FOREVER IN dire need of some kind of help to make the next move, the next advance of my life. If it was not for the special letter of recommendation from my philosophy professor Dr. Williams, I would not have been accepted at the Claremont School of Theology. I look back fondly and gratefully on him just as I look back in the same way on the Reverend Woodruff, the Yosemite chaplain. Both built bridges of transcendence to yonder shore for a person they knew had a spotty record and a tenuous existence in this country. They saw the fog of uncertainty enshrouding the young man's life, but they also witnessed the fire of life in his zesty public campground ministry in the one case and the assiduousness of his class work in the other. They had faith, they must have had, that the young man would in turn someday build bridges for others.

Claremont is a town on the Eastern edge of Los Angeles County. It is the home of a consortium of colleges and graduate school, all private, and of the seminary to which I was admitted. This seminary did not feel cloistered to me. It had just recently opened its doors in that location, and consequently the student body was small and the buildings new and sparse. The architecture and landscaping bespoke cactus and open desert. Mount Baldy loomed to the north as Mount Tamalpais had done in San Anselmo to the west, but the former was dry, rocky, and gulchy.

At that time you passed through orange groves north of Foothill Boulevard on your way up the mountains. Half way up to the ski lifts was the village of Mount Baldy with a handful of bars and restaurants and hamburger stops. At the juke box in one spot you could play Joanie Sommers' hit *Johnny Get Angry*, which I have done more than once over the years. A stream flowed through a landslide of white boulders and a grove of aspens before it came down through the village. Once a spider came down from a limb in the dark grove heading straight for the water, but it changed its mind as it got close to the roaring tumult of spray and foam.

When I attended the seminary there was no dominant theology whose influence infused the school's culture as Barth's had done in San Anselmo, though Professor John Cobb Jr. reminded us in every class of the debt his thinking owed to the process philosophy of Alfred North Whitehead. In the kitchen co-op I remember the dorm chatter was once about the philosophical theologian Paul Tillich, who was at that time University Professor at Harvard. Tillich's loaded metaphysical language about the ground of being, the inexhaustible depth of being, and the courage to be in the face of nonbeing was liberating and endlessly evocative of new ways of being in the world. That we were being exposed to Tillich and Whitehead was a testament to the liberal, open-minded, progressive culture, intentionally fostered, of this new seminary. There was something altogether bright and fresh about this.

Pilgrim, are you breaking away from the Eden of your own sheltered religion? Are you daring to risk the security of your long-held beliefs, be they religious or not, to follow an intuition or growing insight, some new light from a source in church or a book, at work or a retreat? Are you anxious like I was to open up, as a flower to the sun, to new ways of being in the world? Are you perhaps entering the dark night of the soul, like the medieval mystics, to purge it of falsehood and human mockery and bad faith? Would you have the courage to be in the face of nonbeing?

Expect the serpent faces of nonbeing to tempt you and taunt you as you approach the East Gate. One will be well-dressed and try to persuade you of how unfaithful and misled you are. It will call you an infidel and warn you of the wrath to come for you and your loved ones if you depart. It will speak to you of the abyss of condemnation, the despair of excommunication, the hardscrabble life of no rest or redemption, of no hope or welcome east of Eden. You will live in cheap apartments and do hard labor in factories and restaurants and motels, and no one will lift a hand to help liberate your life from poverty and depression.

Another figure will be slimy and coiled. It will scare you and scold you and sentence you to a loveless life, urging, Turn back, O mortal one, before

Mount Baldy

it is too late. Who will love you if you surrender your convictions? Does this not bespeak a failure of nerve? Even your family and best friends will forsake you. You will live as if in a land of famine. It will not be a hunger for bread or a thirst for water, but a want of someone to run to in the evenings and hold tenderly in your arms. You will look from sea to sea, from east to west, you will spend your hours in the clubs and your nights in the cities in search of love, and you will not find it. They will look away, as if to say, Find yourself a life first. They will turn their heads, finding you wanting for inner strength.

Still a third demonic figure was dressed in a black robe and accused me of sin. You are a fool. What is it that drives you from here but your hubristic thoughts by day and thoughts of lustful freedom by night? License leads only to actions that cannot be undone. Your enemies will know this and will take advantage. You will have no exit plan, no defense, no excuse or justification. Savage Death will await you in the ring. Pilgrim, I will tell you later of how Death did await me in the ring, but it was not for my departure from Eden.

In truth, it was with vainglorious pride and brash ignorance that I faced down this last and the other snakelike demons, sure that they would blink in time, and that I would move beyond the second chapter of Genesis and through the raging waters of Exodus. I saw a new world opening up for me in this plush academic town of old eucalyptus trees lining College Avenue, downtown cafes, proud, pampered homes, blithe, colorful students darting about in their new clothes. It was an avant-garde atmosphere electric with art and intellect, and the opportunity for learning seemed endless. I started working in the Honnold Library of the Claremont Colleges and in time came to know some of the young men and women and their colleges. Some of them had rooms next to mine in an old house on Yale Avenue.

In those days much was going on in my spiritual life, though the dawning of the 1960s and this new zeitgeist had me in their thrall and caused me to hold my religion if not my deeper self in abeyance under the surface. I wrote a longish poem, *The Ashram of E. Stanley Jones*, lyricizing my remembered experience with that legendary missionary in the Himalayan foothills. That mountain experience of lakeside vespers, of early morning silence in the round chapel, the singing of *I Shall Not Be Afraid* as we walked in twos to breakfast, and of being mesmerized by the inspiring India and America stories Brother Stanley told in his lectures and sermons, was proving to be rich and sustaining as I went through the valley of tectonic shifts and changes.

The details of Tillich's theology seemed daunting, as did the details of process theology, which was being championed by Professor Cobb. Cobb was a slim, wiry young man of five feet and seven inches or so, with glasses, which he adjusted constantly, and a dense crop of blond hair. He spoke clearly and distinctly, as if he was by principle committed to speak that way. Except for his unabashed southern accent from Georgia, one could see him as a don straight out of Cambridge. Bright and quick, with an easy smile and firm lips, he seemed happy to linger in class and in the sunny courtyard to talk with students, Mount Baldy sparkling with snow overhead in the winter. No one argued with him during his lectures.

I was impressed by the audacity, clarity, and resolve with which Cobb's new book *God and the World* departed both from the religious exclusivism of the Christian tradition, on the one hand, and from the secular purism of modern Western culture, on the other. It rejected the disjunction, Either God or this world, so characteristic of the Kierkegaardian neo-orthodoxy taught at San Anselmo, and affirmed rather the conjunction, Both God and the world. In this, I felt, there was wisdom and courage, but again I was not yet ready to evaluate it and declare the measure of its importance in the realm of ideas. I would need to wait for the right time, when I could survey my experience over the long haul and take stock of the wisdom I might have assimilated over the years.

While I was slow in grasping the Whiteheadian philosophy that powered Cobb's book forward, I applauded the broad, bold, youthful brush strokes of the new conceptual horizon coming suddenly into view, as if we've turned a corner on a winding mountain road. Cobb was such a natural theoretician. He loved taking stratospheric ideas, folding them into his own conscience, and setting them afloat like paper boats downstream, daring to believe that they would change the world.

Something new and splendidly panoramic was happening here, and it had to do with what Tillich and Cobb had in common. Put simply, they were both philosophical theologians. They embraced both philosophy and theology with a fearlessly outspoken, unapologetic, and ardent love. In the previous chapter I spoke of these two different frames of reference and their two respective universes. I sketched how it seemed to be the norm for these universes to move threateningly in opposing directions. Here I was learning that a somewhat friendlier way of understanding a possible marriage between the two disciplines is possible.

In Tillich's case there did remain a certain tension between Biblical religion and the metaphysical search for ultimate reality, a tension which he said we must absorb and within which we must remain serene. In Cobb's case theology was being cradled and grounded carefully in philosophical language. I was beginning to feel that I was in good theological hands, and that I had the support of an important and respected tradition in theology and the companionship of exceptional and robust religious thinkers and teachers. That the general drift of my own theology was the right one for me was now becoming something of an established fact. Deep in my heart I was happy.

The pictures on the wall began finally to fade in resonance, and the old doctrines seemed no longer that compelling. There was, no doubt, the terror of becoming unglued, but this new environment and these new courses in theology, religion, and values at the seminary and at the Claremont Graduate School promised to lead to my wondrous and fearful remaking east of Eden.

I did my Master's thesis on John Dewey, in whom I had a growing interest since Chapman College. Dewey never felt stale, but always full of passion and intelligence. In his simple little paperback *A Common Faith* he propounds the view that the idealism that drives religion can flourish imaginatively without the encumbrances of any particular religion or dogmatic belief. He himself tries in the book to rescue what he sees as vital in religion. God, he says, is exactly the tension between the ideal and the actual, the disequilibrium that drives life forward. I struggled for a long time quietly with his sober and impeccable rendering of secular faith. I was and still am an admirer of Dewey.

In the end I found myself stranded on the border between what Plutarch called the marshes of superstition and the precipice of godlessness. The gusts of irresolution and ambivalence continued their onslaught on the passionate and wayward voyage of a yet determined pilgrim. I worked part-time in the church, and it felt good and right to start graduate work in philosophy at what is now Claremont Graduate University. That both the religious and the secular frames of reference would exist side by side felt auspicious. That I would get to stay under Mount Baldy for a few more years was comforting.

10

Chapter Zero
Lemmon was highpowered and driven, Louch grounded and relaxed

FROM THE START I was afraid of Professor E. J. Lemmon. I did think of this as a purely personal thing with me, though I speculated that his being English and my being Indian was an unconscious factor on both sides. That I was coming straight out of seminary, so I thought, may also have prejudiced him. Was he perchance a cultured despiser of religion? The question crossed my mind, though not in those terms. Be that as it may, since there may not have been such a thing as his side of the story, I'll stay on my side with what I really know.

Lemmon towered above the other philosophy professors at the graduate school. A virtuosic, cutting edge figure, he had something of a following among the brightest students. I certainly did not regard myself as being among them, but I too admired him and followed at a distance. I was afraid of being utterly and completely crushed by the man if I said something that revealed how dumb I actually was. I did not know any logic or any of the brand new methods that the discipline was abuzz with, and Lemmon was an especially good logician and a scrupulous analytical philosopher. I could actually witness this in class by the way he thought on his feet. Could he tell how I sat clammed up at the edge of my seat? Could he sense the power he had?

A tall, intense young man with a broad granite face, he had been a tutor at Oxford for the famous J. L. Austin. The fine points he made, the way everything seemed to puzzle him, it was all new to me. You can see blue, I recall him saying, but blue is a universal. When he strongly urged the study of what he referred to as Chapter Zero of Alonzo Church's *Introduction to Mathematical Logic* for all philosophy students, I went out and bought that book after browsing through it in the library. Church was the distinguished founder and editor of *The Journal of Symbolic Logic*. I was shy in Lemmon's presence but was also galvanized into action. Why could I not learn his skills? Why could not I too become a good philosopher?

Lemmon became human to me when I heard that he had attended the debates on the Vietnam War at one of the colleges. He was not just brains. And it was a sad day when we heard of his sudden death. He had a weak heart, and his student friends should have known better than to take him up ten thousand feet to Mount Baldy. I had just finished auditing his advanced class on formal modal logic, the logic of necessity and possibility, a new area in which he was the world's leading authority. I would sit in the front row and take meticulous notes, having by this time familiarized myself with proofs and theorems and systems from the book by Alonzo Church.

The white dust of Lemmon's new firmament of possible worlds flared up off the blackboard in that classroom in the science building at Pomona College. As I recall, necessity meant access to all possible worlds, possibility to at least one. Lemmon was so unstinting with his knowledge that he became for me a bridge, interestingly enough, to hitherto unconceived possible shores.

It was also Lemmon's influence that led me to J. L. Austin's *Sense and Sensibilia*, a delightful little paperback that packed a seismic wallop. Modern philosophy of knowledge was torn apart piece by piece by exposing the deeply ingrained misuse of words like real, seems, appears, illusion. With dexterity, ease, and even humor the whole edifice of bogus puzzles and problems that Descartes and later philosophers had created was dismantled. Philosophical theories became so deflatable and the figure of Wittgenstein loomed so large in the sky with the same leanings and misgivings that we learned to be modest about what we said and guarded about the way we said it.

Those days in the 1960s were alive for me with giant near-mythic luminaries like Tillich, Whitehead, Austin, Wittgenstein, and Alonzo Church. The marketplace of ideas was buzzing with bold, new pathfinding teachers like Cobb and Lemmon. It happened, oh so gradually, that I was acquiring a small measure of confidence in my abilities. In both theology and philosophy the excitement of learning and the sweet feeling of deep release were in the air.

In theology the world had shifted to make room for philosophy. Cobb's *God and the World* shook with the vibrations of life. Life surges forward, attracted by the divine lure, whether from the floors of the ocean, from nurse logs in primeval forests, from the palettes of painters or the scribblings of poets, or from the apostolic journeys of missionaries and pilgrims, choosing in each case, moment by moment, richer and worthier goods and goals. Cobb's thinking struck the same throbbing, elemental note that I had heard in Hendry and Buber, except that process theology was girded by the full symphony of the story of life itself. The stranglehold of the past is broken. Fluid, relational, evolutionary ideas replace the old atomistic doctrines of impassivity and substance.

In philosophy the linguistic breakthroughs of Austin and Wittgenstein gave us what we needed to sweep out the cobwebs in our own conceptual schemes, to dig ourselves out of dungeons of shadows into the clear light of day. Now we would know the snares in vested ideas, the pitfalls in arguments invidious and laborious. We would learn to think for ourselves. There was a future in the life of reason. If there was some anxiety in this still strange, new world, I could not sense it.

Then came Professor A. R. Louch. He too was an Englishman from Oxford, come now to replace Lemmon and become chairperson of the department. What I saw when I met him for the first time was a darkish man with bushy eyebrows and a glowering demeanor. In time, however, I came to see him as a magnanimous and warm human being. There was a certain depth about him, with no air whatsoever of self-exaggeration. Heidi was an undergraduate who was taking an introductory course from him. She liked him and commented on the nonchalant way he lectured and the homey examples he used.

Around Louch I did not feel like Skinny on the beach against Atlas. Lemmon was highpowered and driven, Louch grounded and relaxed. Unlike Lemmon, Louch showed no fondness for symbolic logic and was not given to making use of it in his own work. Secretly I rejoiced in his independence and breathed a sigh of relief. Louch had a mind of his own. An important lesson was transpiring right there in front of me. There was more than one way of being a philosopher. You could be yourself.

Chapter Zero

Louch's book *Explanation and Human Action* made no stunning breakthroughs but guided the reader through the philosophy of mind and of action using examples rather than overarching theories. In the tradition of Austin and Wittgenstein the book decried the supposed unbridgeable gulf between fact and value, insisting that while human actions are certainly factual events, they are best understood as belonging in a broadly moral category. The book was against sweeping generalizations and pseudo-scientific explanations at a time when the philosophy of science, with its deductive models of human behavior, was a growing trend. In a movie a man on a bicycle is seen from a distance swinging his arms wildly in the air. The lookers-on are puzzled. The man gets closer. There is a bee.

What a cacophony of worlds my life had become. There was the academic world. I filled several notebooks, intended for Lemmon before he died, with exercises from Alonzo Church. The masterful way Church explained even the most complex topic made the next topic accessible and inviting, and I resolved to work far beyond the introductory Chapter Zero and deep into the book as far as I could go. Never in my life had I ever entered such an elevated, self-contained world of elegance and abstraction.

As if the differences between Lemmon, Louch, and Cobb were not instructive enough for my spiritual journey, there was the world of church, through which I was employed. I lived for a while in Pasadena and worked part-time there in the First Congregational United Church of Christ with youth and young adults when the church was between ministers, commuting to Claremont for my classes.

On occasion I got to preach, and I found that a rich store of spiritual and theological resources from my remote and recent past had accumulated beneath the surface. I could see that I was a naturally good preacher, and I felt comfortable working in a church where no fuss was made over doctrine. A charming elderly woman, distinguished in appearance and manner, and active in the Pasadena Parents and Teachers Association, was the Director of Christian Education. She and I went from room to room upstairs in that colossus of a creaky building talking of how we could incorporate great art into our educational program.

In the decentralizing world of male and female I learned how to ask a woman out for a date. One Claremont student, who I will call Ann, was playful and patient, had a happy, round face, and was a French major who loved Baudelaire and endured my laughter when she mispronounced Descartes. She would say, Love is not fifty-fifty but hundred-hundred. I hated it, though, when the Lebanese guy would come around at the Coop with his copy of *The Prophet*. She swooned over him and the book, and I ceased to exist. She swooned over a visiting Scottish young man too in the Harvard cafe, but I admit that he was strikingly handsome.

My father came to visit me and my younger brother, who had come to the United States two years after me. My father had Presbyterian connections in the Los Angeles area, and it was fun driving him and my brother to Wilshire Boulevard and down the Pacific Coast Highway and eating hamburgers at Big Boy's and A & W Root beer everywhere. When asked later in India what he remembered from his trip, he said, of all things, Two bucks regular.

11

Kierkegaard's Truth
I go to be hanged on yonder gallows

When my work at the Pasadena church ended, I ceased to have any connection with religion. I did not know much better at the time. The fact was that I had a floundering personal faith and little wisdom about the living of life. I had little money, no roots or permanent standing in the United States, and something of a tumbling tumbleweed of an identity. The church would have provided a spiritual anchor, a supportive community, a moral compass. Instead, I traded my birthright for a mess of pottage. Comparing myself to the other students at the elite Claremont Colleges was like comparing myself to the students at St. Stephens College in Delhi. I stood out as a commoner. I felt socially tainted and existentially prayerless.

Even my relationship with my girlfriend Ann felt temporary and one-sided from the start, as if I knew all along where I stood. It was after her second year, I think, that she left Claremont and returned to her home state, where she would continue her studies. She did invite me to come and visit her and her family. I took the bus and stayed at their home for a week in the summer. I had become emotional about her and asked her to marry me. I'm far too young for marriage, she explained, quite rightly, in her small room. I looked at her with wet eyes from the bus as I began the long journey home on Route 66 back to California. I remember stopping in Albuquerque. There was a big railway junction and standing trains without an engine. It brought back memories.

The only meaning and order I had in my life came from my graduate studies, in which I was doing fairly well. In my sleek spaceship of three axioms I toured in sobered awe the starry firmament of theorems at the outer edges of the solar system. Better than having your own Hubble telescope was being right there just a handful of light years away from the next galaxy.

It was back in the introductory Chapter Zero, however, that Plato entered my universe in a big way. Abstract forms such as Justice, Truth, Beauty, and Goodness are to be distinguished from the measurable, tangible entities that are imperfect instances of them. The form Justice is to be distinguished from particular just societies, whose justice might be impaired by, say, a tradition of gender inequality. The form Life is to be distinguished from particular living beings, which are its instances. We will have more to say about this particular form and its instances later. Church admits being influenced by the German logician Gottlob Frege, who was a Platonist through and through.

Chapter Zero explains and justifies the foregoing distinction in an interesting way. Roughly, it proceeds by distinguishing between the concrete denotation of a term and the intellectual meaning or connotation of that term. The name "Sir Walter Scott" denotes the same flesh and blood person as the description "the author of Waverly," but these expressions have different intellectual significations. In the former we have the idea of a knight or baronet having such and such a first and last name, but in the latter we have just that the person wrote Waverly. Thus the concrete denotation of a term, in this case the person who wrote the Waverly novels, is seen to be a different reality from its abstract, intellectual meaning, the connotation that is grasped when we understand the term.

Abstract meanings were said by Church and Frege to be concepts. For Plato they were forms. Elsewhere in the literature they are known as universals and attributes. I did wonder whether the Eternal Thou is in fact the Eternal and Universal Thou. If so, I would already have an answer to the God question. God would thus be understood as an abstraction, and particular Thous would be infinitely small, imperfect instances of God, sparks out of the Divine Fire. This became and remained an open and burning question for me for years and years. Still again, to make my own decision I would need to wait for the fullness of time.

I must note in passing that while an important thought had been planted in my mind and soul about God and abstract objects, it was even more important that I was being taught how to think. We learn by example,

Kierkegaard's Truth

and I was fortunate to count Alonzo Church as being among my best examples.

The Platonist view was not a popular one among the preeminent philosophers of the time, who tended to be nominalists and radical empiricists. Willard van Orman Quine, Morton White, and other influential philosophers offered alternate understandings of meaning. As I matured I became more and more convinced of the shallowness and inadequacy of their proposals.

Even as I was enlightened and gladdened by the above discoveries, it was Kierkegaard's truth about the proneness of reason and religion to lose consonance with existential realities that had come to rule my world. While reason is certainly a reliable guide for existence, it can and does often happen in churches, monasteries, and academic establishments that the higher self is tragically unresponsive to the needs of existence, like a man so preoccupied with his own agenda that over the years he neglects his marriage and does not heed the voice of his wife yelling, outside the farmhouse, The barn is burning! The barn is burning!

Existence in turn, like a child, will often demand attention from intellect and distract, distort, and undermine it. To be sure, existence can intervene justifiably in the gated gardens of knowledge. This is just the reason why Sartre had pronounced existence as being prior to essence. Had not Kierkegaard cast legitimate doubts on the secure religiousness of Bishop Mynster? Yet cravings, addictions, and obsessions have been known to drag the higher self down into the gutter. Do not Sin and Death prowl in the garden of the knowledge of good and evil? And now even over Alonzo Church's pages of pure reason loomed the shadow of a gallows.

I came across this story that Church gives as an exercise. When Sancho Panza was governor of Barataria, there was in a certain manor a river with a bridge, on the one end of which was a gallows. A law had been enacted whereby whoever crossed the bridge must first swear whither he was going and why. If he swore truthfully he would be allowed to cross, and if falsely he would be hanged. Now one person came and swore, I go to be hanged on yonder gallows, and proceeded to cross the bridge. The vexed question came before Sancho Panza as to whether the person should be hanged. Church then asks us to verify the complex tautology which says that the law cannot be upheld in this instance.

The existential reality is, of course, that the person may still be hanged. There is also the strange special case of the person who came to the bridge and swore, I come to love a pretty college woman, and proceeded to cross the bridge petrified that he may not be able to keep his promise. I had been drawn from a distance to the woman whom I will call Katherine, and had finally asked her to come and see *Dr. Zhivago* with me at the Grauman's Chinese. I was soon to learn that I should have established an I and Thou friendship with her before jumping into such a big evening. Yes, deep down I was already afraid.

Katherine was warm and personable, and my sky blue Chevy Impala with its beautiful fins streaked up the Covina and Forest Lawn Cemetery hills, slinked past the slower cars, hummed through the Los Angeles interchange, and powered itself onto the Hollywood Freeway with grace and speed, pulling into the right lane after Santa Monica Boulevard. Never has a car been so proud, transported such beauty, and performed so dutifully. But Katherine sat an ocean away on the passenger side, and I did not reach for her. It went that way all evening, even through the tears of Lara's Theme, *Somewhere my love, there will be songs to sing*.

Somewhere, my love, there will be songs, yes, and I must leave you with those borrowed words. I had elevated you into something of an aesthetic prize. I had turned you into an idol, a bronze serpent in my desert of desperation. How I would pull you close in the car, but how fragile my heart. I would offer you my hand at the movies, but how tormented my spirit. I would give you my arms in the darkness of my apartment, but how impotent my soul. I had not lied, but I had indeed sworn falsely at the bridge.

Why does this small incident vex me so? Why do I waste your precious time, Pilgrim, with my private anarchy? Bear with me, fellow traveler, and let us listen to that lovely award-winning song from *Dr. Zhivago* on my stereo, for I want you to hear my story, and hear it musically, as I myself hear it in my heart. The song will find resonance in the poignancy of your own story as well, which you will tell me, for someone may come to you too out of the long ago. And in the song's hearing, we will brood with each other about life, how deserted an avenue can become after the evening shadows fall, how lifeless a town can be, how cold and loveless the streets outside our windows can appear, and how the only sound track so often is composed of the chords of sadness and loss.

12

Kurukshetra

*They've given you a number, and
taken 'way your name*

No, I was not the silver-tongued, stonefaced commander of my own life, the invincible one who owes no one anything, who owns a Corvette and drives away with the pretty dark-eyed graduate student next door who uses words like obsequious. My ship was anchored in my studies, but I was swimming far out in the sea of life. The purism and piety, the memories of missionaries and family prayers, and now even the church and its sermons and hymns, and my theological probing for impenetrable meanings under every stone and uncontrollable mysteries on the bestial floor were all in the waiting, as if they were sure I would come full circle and find a way to be reconciled in my end times, when other helpers fail and comforts flee.

To compensate for my poison cup of futility in love, I segued into delusions of grandeur and strong opinions. Not as a Dr. Strangelove about to blow the world to smithereens, but as the intrepid Dr. Zero, alias Dr. Theo, concocting in my philosophico-theological lab the perfect antidote for my bitter cup of existential troubledness, a Truth Potion #9 that would sway the hearts and minds of women and men all over the world. My old college friends Gilchrist and Mohit would be part proud and part jealous of me. Soon I would rule the world and earn the respect of the girl of my dreams. She would wait for me like the bride in *High Noon*, and I would dance with her to *Why Do the Birds Keep on Singing?*, *Soldier Boy*, and *Surfer Girl* in the face of the staring crowd. It was my deepest secret, this masquerade.

The Meaning of These Days

Temperamentally and by background I was not a political person like my friend Mike had been in Orange. He was from a newspaper family in Seattle and spoke fluidly about the Eisenhower years, of Nixon and China and Adlai Stevenson and Governor Brown. It was impossible, however, not to pick up the social tensions of those days, the cold war, Vietnam, the civil rights and peace movements, the flower children. Rebellions and revolutions were hatched on street corners, in coffee houses, in employment agencies.

The strain of melancholy found expression in *Where Have All the Flowers Gone* and *Abraham, Martin, and John*. Johnny Rivers sang his *Secret Agent Man* of the television series at the Whiskey A-Go-Go. The lyrics, "They've given you a number, and taken 'way your name. . ..Odds are you won't live to see tomorrow," were not so much sad, however, as they were abandonment and the embrace of the mean streets. Bob Dylan expressed the fecundity and serendipity of the times brilliantly with lines like, "The answer, my friend, is blowing in the wind."

One answer came at me in the form of a scream. The woman –a short, dark-haired woman, who often wore loose, colorful, ankle-length dresses— and her husband, a fellow graduate philosophy student and a soft-spoken and refined young man, were my neighbors.. They had been thoughtful enough to have me over for dinner once. We were standing and chatting on the street casually about the war in Vietnam. I admit that I was not up-to-the-minute on developments, and I was oblivious to the fact that her husband could be drafted and oblivious to how my being a noncitizen and exempt from the draft might be playing in her mind.

She screamed at me. It was about the folly of the war and the wasteful diversion of her husband's time and resources from his graduate studies. It was about the principalities and powers in high places. It was also, I'm afraid, about my own insouciance in the face of the deepening shadow in which she and her husband lived. I was shaken, and I was moved by her guardianship of her husband's life. I had heard that scream before, the scream of the woman on the bridge in my first philosophy book. The answer blowing in the wind was not academic but existential.

Not all answers, however, were blowing in the wind. The philosopher Morton White's answer to the outraged young who sit in or drop out was that while his heart goes out to them, he finds them repeating the mistake of Ralph Waldo Emerson, who had failed to see that in perilous times we must lean not on the oracles of the heart alone, but also on the counsel of the mind and the testimony of our senses. We are whole thinking and feeling and sensing beings, admonished White, and we must lean on our minds and our senses as well as on our hearts.

The answers that blow in the wind are those born of the travail of the soul. They are Truths that are big and full and existential, and midwifed, yes, by the whole thinking, feeling, and sensing self. Were the sitting in and dropping out youth truly making the mistake that White alleges? I do not think so. Surely their Truth was in the same neighborhood as that of Martin Luther King Jr. and of Gandhi. Surely they were in revolt, not just emotionally but intellectually and sensuously as well, against the establishment's brightest and best pursuing war, blind capitalism, and other policies dangerous to the environment and to living beings. And was not their Truth born, like my neighbor's scream and like the indignities suffered by King and Gandhi, of the consternation of the soul? Was not just this the reason why their Truth was borne, like a beautiful balloon, upon the four winds?

Gandhi was, of course, well-versed in the *Bhagavad Gita*, which is a philosophico-theological episode in the *Mahabharata* epic about two related but warring families, and which contains the moral and spiritual instructions given by Krishna to Arjuna on the battlefield of Kurukshetra. Gandhi interpreted Kurukshetra as the soul, and the epic battle as the war between good and evil. The answers embraced by the young were of a piece with those of Gandhi. They were of the mind and the senses as well as of the heart, and they were changing the world.

Well-known by now is also that Gandhi's Truth was not born in a science lab or in a philosophy class. I was in the Sat Tal ashram when, in a sermon by Brother Stanley, I first heard that *satyagraha*, truth force, was birthed, if not conceived, on a chilly platform in the Petermaritzburg railway station. There Gandhi brooded on his ejection from his first-class compartment on the train to Pretoria because he was, as the conductor had said, colored.

Gandhi responded to his ejection with his whole mental, physical, and emotional being. He was in Kurukshetra, the battle between good and evil was raging, and his black frock coat, the striped trousers, and the other layers of socialization were of no avail to help him sort things through and decide what to do. But John Stuart Mill's *On Liberty*? Yes. The Sermon on the Mount? Yes. The *Bhagavad Gita*? Yes. Henry David Thoreau on civil disobedience? Yes. Midwifed by thought, outrage, and what strength the thin man had, Gandhi's Truth was born, and it would soon be aloft in the wind and inscribed on the front pages of newspapers in the four corners of the earth.

With respect to answers that blow in the wind, like those of Gandhi, the disillusioned youth, and Martin Luther King Jr., whose Truth also stemmed from a long history of deep hurts and injustices, there is no space for intellectual or political wrangling. The need instead is for prophets, preachers, and poets, for people of faith to fill the places of worship and prayer, for dream speeches and songs. The big answers are simple answers. I once was blind, but now I see. We shall overcome. The Truth shall set us free. The answers are always as good and big as their melodies.

One answer has been trapped in my heart forever, and I must set it free to fly upon the wind. It is yet another small truth about my own yellow brick road of ambivalence and indecision, and often of making the wrong decisions. A young woman in Philosophy 101 at the University of California at Riverside submitted a long poem as a term paper. It was inappropriate for that class. We had been reading Plato's *Republic* all semester, and I was the teaching assistant for her section. After Chapter Zero I had come to appreciate Plato's dialogues and definitions. I talked with her about the low grade I was compelled to give her, acknowledging that she had put deep thought and feeling into her poem. She received what I said gracefully and quietly. There was no expression on her face as she stood up to leave.

I was the one who walked away with a heavy heart. There was no reversing what I had done, nor any Truth in it, I felt, not in the big sense. I had even possibly transgressed beyond some sacred boundary into a bloodless I-It land with no memory of I-Thou. Tell me, Pilgrim, how you feel. Had I violated some unfathomable, primordial trust? A love as silent and unspeakable as the coming out of stars in the evening when the day is done?

13

The Tahquamenon
I will arise and go now, and go to Inisfree

I STARTED SEEING A woman about my own age, a woman I will call Mariah to protect her identity. An acquaintance introduced me to her in a diner. She had no religious background whatsoever and was a conscientious and diligent atheist. She did introduce me to poetry, and that is how I became familiar with the poems of W. B. Yeats. She was tenderly close to her mother and her sister's family, and we shared the love of music, the blues albums of Muddy Waters, Nina Simone, and others playing frequently in her apartment. She was literate and spoke intelligently and compassionately about the mentally ill and the poor, with whom she worked professionally.

I felt quite close to her and actually came, at some deeper level, to admire her. It was more than just her advocacy for the socially marginalized. It was the sweet, singular affection and bonding she felt for her sister and her family, who I came to know as well, that worked its way into my bloodstream. Family was something I had become hardened about over my own years of railway station departures in the plains and bus terminal arrivals in the clouds, but Mariah's tokens and gestures of endearment seemed authentic, and the cold, cold heart of unmeaning began to yield to a deeper, warmer self. We saw *Goldfinger* and *The Graduate* at the Grauman's Chinese. We hiked on Mount Baldy and ran down one of the steep, rocky gulches with abandon holding hands. We read poetry and talked philosophy.

Mariah's voice was light and soft, and it became musical in the diner when she recited lines like, "I will arise and go now, and go to Inisfree." The

Billie Holliday fragility in her voice had a strange power over me. I learned, furthermore, how afflicted she was by psychosomatic, springback abdominal pains, used prescribed codeine and barbiturates, and withdrew when an attack occurred into the bedroom or bathroom while a blues album of B. B King played on the stereo. She seemed to have no other resource than this to treat her ailment, though she had a doctor.

Our relationship deepened gradually, though not without a series of disturbing incidents, in and through which I almost recoiled for good, involving her prior relationships. Loyalty prevailed, and eventually, since it is impossible not to imagine and anticipate the future, marriage felt to both of us like the next logical step. The skimpy, unadorned wedding occurred in her sister's home, and after the saying of our vows Mariah grew faint and had to lie down for a while.

How much did Mariah know in the cells of her being when she fell, I wonder, or was it just that her constitution was not as strong as mine? Did she know the lines we were disavowing of our own ground in order to meet half way on our bridge? Did she know the magnitude of the risk she and I were taking? Did she know my limitations as well as her own? Was it Fear that appeared suddenly as a phantom and delivered a blow to her head, causing her to swoon?

Did it just dawn on her that we were from two entirely different shores, and how narrow and rickety the bridge we ourselves had made, how far the cedars looked now on the ridge, how wide and deep the river flowing far down below us, how swift and strong its currents, that can chill the bone, crush the soul to powder, and break the heart to pieces? Did she know that we were doing this because there seemed no other choice for two desperately lonely persons who had come to find in each other companionship, safe harbor, and some common cause? That this was the nature of love and life?

We moved into a new apartment complex just north of Foothill Boulevard and were happy together, Mariah, me, the old terrier Sammy, and the two cats we acquired, Iona and Cuchalain, named by Mariah after figures in Irish mythology. Iona was sleek, silver-haired, and cheetah-looking, and Cuchulainn a mustard-colored rotund tabby. A longhaired black injured cat also began to live with us. Mariah named him Dmitri, after the character in *The Brothers Karamazoff*, but we had to put him to sleep eventually. Cuchulainn would jump on me early in the morning and nose me awake

The Tahquamenon

to try and tell me something. Our neighbors had declawed cats who felt unsafe when left outside even in the small yard enclosed by a wooden fence.

Mariah made sure that our cats were all neutered or spayed and got proper veterinary care. A larger-than-life overpowering, unneutered Siamese cat ruled all the alleys, fences, parks, and streets in cat city at night. I saw him once, I remember, on the fence in our backyard at night. He was well-fed and big, and scary like a bobcat. I suspected him of having injured the hungry and homeless Dmitri before we rescued him from the orange grove next to the apartments, between which there was again no fence. He was just sitting there wounded under an orange tree when we scooped him into the cage.

Suddenly, it seemed, I had stepped into a fairyland world of household, marriage, family, and pets. I was surprised by how fulfilling and fun this could be. It brought stability to a life that had known no stability. It brought love to a person who had grasped in vain for love and knew not its meaning. Sweet rain was falling and streams were flowing in a barren and rocky land of hot Santa Ana winds and drought and coyotes in the brown hills, a Biblical wilderness. The fanged figures of Sin and Death withdrew into the orange groves, the blue oaks, and the ravines. With my now being disaffiliated from the church, had Sin already done its poisonous work? Would Death now simply bide its time? Were the streams in the desert a mirage?

I had done quite well in philosophy, though I still had my dissertation to do. I began searching for a fulltime teaching position. A church career was no longer an option. For Mariah it would have been dissimulative and professionally inferior, but it was our joint decision that religion would have no place on our bridge. For her, religion was unthinkable.

What was I thinking? That religion would still be on hold? Suppressed for me, as if in a reserve fund? Yes. That I still had unfinished business with it? Yes. That philosophy, Mariah, and I were doing well together, and why ruin a good thing? Yes. Could I have chosen, nonetheless, to maintain my association with church and continue my interest in theology? Yes, I could have done so even before I met Mariah, but now my religion would have been a fragmented, ungodly, and impotent thing off to the side, and it would have altered our relationship.

Furthermore, was there not meaning enough in philosophy and the new life I had with Mariah? Was not this new way of being an experiment that I felt worth trying? Was I giving away my power to Mariah? Again, I had already given away my power. There was an underlying sense of just drifting through on the streets of Laredo. I was a tumbleweed that day on the road to anywhere.

Our first major decision was to move to Atlanta, where I had been accepted as an assistant professor in a university. I could find no philosophy jobs in California, where we both wanted to remain. In Mariah's red Volkswagen bug we traveled first to Michigan where her mother lived in the cold and clean and beautiful north with a big malamute and a cat. There was a natural childlike quality in the way Mariah related to her mother so embracingly and happily, and it felt good and affirming to be introduced to her now. In the evening the three of us played Scrabble. Once I had to persuade my mother-in-law by citing examples that "militaries" is in fact a word.

Mariah and I took a break and ferried to Mackinac Island, the perimeter of which we bicycled, and then we went further north to the Hiawatha National Forest in Upper Michigan. After hiking on the trail through the thick hardwood forest along the river from Upper Tahquamenon Falls to Lower Tahquamenon Falls, I started worrying at the gift shop there about making it back before dark.

Ten or fifteen minutes into the way back it was getting dark. The roots of the gargantuan old-growth trees reached across the trail toward the river on the left and tripped us, slowing our pace. Darkness fell, and it was easy to lose our way, which we did several times. The only light was the moon in the river, which became our guide. We inched our way hand in hand, keeping as close as we could to the shoreline without trampling into the swampy areas. I was frightened in this forest like never before, but especially because of Mariah I remained composed and steady, groping my way forward. My fear snapped like a twig when we heard the strumming of a banjo and singing approaching us. The group headed downstream told us we were close.

14

Springer Mountain
Consciousness Three was blowing in the wind

WE RENTED A HOUSE just off of Briarcliff Road. The owners instructed us expressly not to trim the azaleas because one just doesn't trim rhododendrons. I had become attached to Los Angeles and southern California, but now I found myself embracing lush green Atlanta with its magnolias, rhododendrons, hollies, redbuds, camellias, dogwoods, and tulip trees. The camellia winter flowers have such a tremblingly delicate aura about them, and there is an inscrutable and fleeting Zen meaning they convey against the dark green on a cold and grey day.

I eventually took to visiting Stone Mountain frequently. Mariah and I also frequented Callaway Gardens a few hours away, the north Georgia mountain forests, where we would rent a Forest Service cabin with a fireplace, and the Smoky Mountains National Park, where we hiked the Appalachian Trail, whose southern terminus is still Springer Mountain, though there are plans to extend the trail. There is a spring there, and I later drank the cold water that trickles down out of the roots and rocks and moss.

My colleagues in the Department of Philosophy were generally congenial and capable. The tenured star of the Department was a young deferential man who was almost feminine in his good looks. Especially bright, balanced, clearheaded, and fairminded, there was the look of success and upward mobility, a natural poise, in his talk and walk. He dressed smartly and wore his stature modestly. To avoid using his real name, I will call him Anthony.

The Meaning of These Days

The colleague I felt closer to, however, had only a Master's degree and, as I recall, was supposed to be working on his Doctorate. I will call him Mark. He was wiry, gaunt, and had a serious, pointed look. He had a Fidel beard, spoke softly and gently, dressed frequently in fatigues, and taught his classes conversationally, outside on a nice day. To talk to him was to talk about Gandhi and Martin Luther King, Jr. and Che Guavara and the whole gauntlet of liberation and human rights and peace concerns.

Mark had the darndest courage to be in the teeth of nonbeing. The old boys' club administration was feeling more and more like circling sharks, what with the war intensifying in Vietnam, the civil rights and peace movement demonstrations making headlines, and the recessionary budget-cutting pressures coming down the pike. Don't step out of line, don't speak out of turn, don't ask a question out loud. That was the sombre, funereal mood as we walked into the plenary faculty meetings.

In his classes and our departmental colloquia Mark connected Western philosophy to what was happening under our noses. An outspoken prophet dwelling in the wilderness at the Jordan, he hammered out justice, proclaimed how the times were a-changing, and how Consciousness Three was blowing in the wind. What he said matched what was happening on the streets and what was being discussed in colleges and coffee shops across the nation. A Marxist student was agitated and all but denounced my raising the traditional mind-body problem as something to be seriously considered in class. She knew in advance that the mind was simply part of the material body, end of matter. She was a bright student and had been in my logic class earlier that year. I did not know that she was a Marxist and an activist.

In those days *The New Yorker* was publishing excerpts from Charles Reich's *The Greening of America*, according to which Consciousness Two had subordinated the human spirit to economics, technology, science, the state, the law, and military power. Loneliness, alienation, and the large-scale destruction of the environment, of human community, and of the sources of meaning and value had been the result. The Consciousness Three of the younger generation was seeking to restore a humane and spiritual existence which respects nature and returns us to the love of landscape. Here was Buber's I and Thou again, and I loved what I was hearing from Mark.

The irony was pointed out by Mark of how the columns of the new Consciousness in *The New Yorker* were being printed side by side with glossy advertising for diamonds and furs, resorts and real estate, cruises and Cadillacs, ivy league education, corporations and financial services, the newest gadgets in technology.

Mark became for me a natural example and teacher. He had a self, a voice. Why did I not myself speak truth to power? It was the question now that blew in the wind when Mark was around. He looked at me in the hallway and all but asked it out loud. He was one who was aware of my seminary background, and the unspoken question on his face was deafening. It tried to broaden my frame of reference, but it was an impossible burden. I was already stretched trying to navigate my way through my dissertation, my marriage, and this new profession of teaching. A voice was saying, Thou, but I did not engage.

Was it not my choice, furthermore, to do philosophical analysis? To explore the conceptual landscape of the Platonic world of logos? Why must I mediate, like Mark, between the ivory tower of forms and the asphalt streets of unrest? It was to the credit of Mark that this last question flared up for me and would not be extinguished. A voice in the wilderness said, Cry, and I gave no answer.

Philosophy, said Heidegger, is untimely, and its echoes in time are dangerous. The administration might well have seen Mark as dangerous and demanded his head. Mark knew this, but he was audacious and confrontational toward the powers that be, and between the lines you could almost hear, "You brood of vipers, who warned you of the wrath to come?" Bear fruit that befits repentance. And I? I was conflicted. I had responsibilities. I worried about Mariah, who had not finished her Master's. I was still working on my dissertation. I had also to consider that I was not a citizen. Still, I felt unmanly. A voice called my name in the cool of the evenings, and I hid behind the trees.

In the meantime, Anthony's influence on me was growing. I envied his rootedness, his fine upbringing. His worldly knowledge of people and culture was impressive, and he talked eloquently about music and art. I asked him how I could get started with classical music, and in his southern drawl he recommended a Brahms and a Tchaikovsky symphony and referred me to an album that had recordings of both. I bought the album and played it often. His future in the institution was assured in a way that Mark's was not. Survival was an elemental theme rife in the four corners of my life. I was like my father, one eye at all times on the raging waters.

If Mark had a self and a voice and Anthony the completeness of a smooth pebble, what was I? Half buried beneath the rubble of a construction site. I had a double life. I was guarded about my seminary background in this controlled, perfectly secular, pumped-in chilly air. Talk about my theological training could raise questions about my standing as a philosopher and my long-range professional goals, questions about which I myself was insecure. The old battle between philosophy and theology was yet waiting to be resolved in Kurukshetra, the human soul. Creeping anxiety and doubt can gnaw at you on the inside and vibrate out nonverbally like soundwaves.

In my marriage, too, the religious question was met with disdain, and I kept it just outside my own reach. Religion was my secret treasure hidden deep under the sea like a sunken ship, to be used if and when the time came. Religion was my power. Religion was my secret rhododendron tree.

I have had many secrets in my life. When I was a boy in boarding school, I had a secret rhododendron tree on a gently sloping hillside of clay soil. Its bark was beige and soft to the touch and flaky, and it had big red flowers in the spring. The place was not dark and dense with shrubs and trees, but open to the light and soft and inviting. When my beloved aunt Ta in Ferozepore would send me a parcel of Indian sweets, I would take them to the rhododendron tree and eat them there. I loved that hillside and that tree and went there often.

Pilgrim, do you have a place where you go to be alone, perhaps for solace, or to write in your journal, to open a letter or parcel and devour what you have received? Or to make an important decision, or simply to brood and just be at that place in peace? It need not be a secret place like my gentle hillside with the rhododendron tree. It could be a place where people can find you if they need you.

15

Peachtree Street
I cover the waterfront, I'm watching the sea

I FINALLY FINISHED MY dissertation on the subject of human action. I chose that topic because, having himself written a book on the subject, Professor Louch could then become the chairperson of my committee. Morton White's book, *The Foundations of Historical Knowledge* had also just appeared, and it provided my research with fresh, up-to-date material. I would read that book chapter by chapter aloud at times to Mariah at night. White was not just a specialist. He could think analytically but also always seemed to have a sense for the history and the larger marketplace of ideas. His writings had implications that reverberated across many streams and valleys. Even his scholarly books were of interest for the general reader.

Mariah acquired her Master's degree at about the same time that I got my Ph.D, which was also at about the time I became a United States citizen. Fortunately, I had memorized the names of the justices on the Supreme Court from an article I had just read in Time Magazine. I telegrammed my father about these happy events, and I heard back from him immediately of his own elation. Soon after this, he and two other family members came to visit us. We took them to Stone Mountain, and we also went to see *Jaws*. The theater was crowded, and I sat next to my father.

Important milestones had passed for both Mariah and me despite the political upheaval and economic recession of those times. They were heartless times, with families under increasing social pressure and financial hardship, people being laid off, and services being cut for the mentally ill. Many patients were discharged from professional care and left to fend for themselves in what was referred to as the community. This was the beginning of homelessness as we know it today, the *reductio ad absurdum* of unbridled capitalism. Mariah and I talked at length and grieved about what she was seeing at the facilities where she worked.

We woke up in the morning to albums by folk singers and I wrote sad poetry. We both loved Joni Mitchell's breakthrough album *Both Sides Now*. The lead song got to me, with its "rows and flows of angel hair, and ice cream castles in the air." Joan Baez sang plaintive songs, like the one about diamonds and rust, and Judy Collins invited a weary sojourner, "Take off your thirsty boots and stay for a while," and she sang a song about Suzanne by the river feeding on tea and oranges from China, the sun pouring down like honey, and how Jesus was a sailor who spent a long time watching from a lonely wooden tower. The songs had a melancholy feel about them, as if they were the last gasp of I and Thou.

Bob Dylan's *It's All Over Now, Baby Blue* was probably among his brightest and best songs. We bought *Abbey Road* too, which I played more than Mariah did, and other albums by The Beatles. I especially liked John Lennon's *Across the Universe*, echoing as it did the dusky, OM-like strains of an Indian ballad. Those songs conveyed the zeitgeist of that era with preternatural beauty. They were about loss, about something primal and precious being taken away forever and ever. They were True in the big sense, and their Truth had melodies. I added Lennon's *Imagine* to this requiem.

The big living room had a maroon carpet, and it was lit up by the opulent colors of azaleas in full bloom in the spring. The screened porch was fun in the summer, and it expanded the room to the side and let in more light. The sun flowed down like honey upon this family of a man, a woman, two cats, and an old dog. We played Billie Holliday and Bessie Smith too. Mariah liked the forlorn, *I Cover the Waterfront* quality of the former, and I was more impressed with the dance rhythms, carnival stylings, and imperial voice of the latter.

It would have to wait for much later when I would grasp what the depressing poetry I wrote and the sad songs I played had to do with my own condition and situation. There was an elemental kind of lostness in the Tahquamenon darkness with only the moon in the river as guide before the banjo came and the singing. Was it an omen that that incident occurred soon after our marriage began? What was going to happen to Mariah and me now? Again, I was afraid.

There was also the matter that I was ineligible for promotion in the Department. I had been working on my dissertation and had done no publishing, and the warning signs about the recessionary and budgetary pressures being felt by institutions of higher education nationally had grown more and more ominous of late. These were the same constraints that were leading to the cuts in social services for the mentally disabled.

For years now I had put all my resources into the learning, doing, and teaching of philosophy, only to run up against the requirement to publish articles, regardless of their human content or depth. Was it all for naught? I did not think so. It had taught me how to think on my own two feet. It had finally given me some actual confidence in my abilities. The big question, however, was looming large now: Should I continue with my philosophical career, given the current recession, and given also my questions and doubts about the ivory tower? In time I could find another job teaching, and could doubtless publish scholarly articles.

Or should I explore work finally in the church, for which I was now lonelier and readier than ever? Every time I passed a church on Ponce de Leon or Peachtree Street the babe leapt in the womb, and a voice inside said, You belong here. You have the chance now to reclaim your lost journey. Feel the earth shift. Hear the message upon the four winds blow. Hear your dry bones come together, the shoulder bone with the neck bone. Hear yourself sing in this valley of defeat. See yourself in a robe, in the pulpit. All the meaning is inside that church. There is food for the hungry, shelter for the homeless, a haven for the shipwrecked, community for the lonely. Here, take back your power.

I approached the judicatory of a mainline denomination and started a dialogue group between some of my college students and the members of an inner city church of that denomination, and I helped out in Sunday morning worship. I was back. The Black church people were like my aunts and uncles in India, with the same skin colorings, the same pictures on the wall, and the same cute cousins. I was back, though the dialogue could not work for too long, given the conservative religiousness of that church and the philosophical wisdom that I myself was trying to foster in my middle class White students. Both sides looked to me with questions when the conversation stalled. What could I say?

As impatient as I was to plunge into the nurture of religious community and narrative, to continue the story that had ended in California, I certainly would not relinquish what I had learned in philosophy. Pilgrim reader, do you see the Golden Gate Bridge between philosophy and religion, the seminary and the city, and intellect and existence coming again into view? It is the bridge of transcendence trying to get built again to a yonder shore.

It felt right to be in solidarity with those who had long been on the margins, to sit at an ecumenical potluck supper and hear Catholic missionaries speak out about the violence and the hunger in Latin America. A wall hanging challenged us to avow our own hunger. It was good to take my place in worship with its reinterpretations of scripture and its "Abide with me, fast falls the eventide," even though the dissonance between pure reason and practical reality, between the idea of dialogue and the manifest diversity of human manner and condition and background, of temperament and religious tradition and level of education, was something I had already come to embrace as an axiom. The opposition seemed ingrained in the human constitution and foreshadowed things to come.

In times of soul-searching, as we reach deeper and deeper into the questions of what we shall do, where we shall go, or even who we are, it might occur to us that we can choose opposite worlds, that we must not be afraid of their possible collision, and that life, far from abhorring oppositions, in fact demands them, and requires that we build a bridge across the wide Missouri. In such times we lean on experience and intuition and instinct as much as on intellect, because the former are likely to be inclusive of the diverse voices within us, and to recall us to the many sides of the mountain. It was Whitehead who emphasized that such choosing of a richer, more abundant good is the essence of the creative process.

I was on the right course this time, embracing both lofty thought and the eventide vespers of the spiritual quandary. The battle raged in Kurukshetra, the human soul, whose soundtrack intones the chasm, even the clash, between the heaven of logos and the travail of creation. The cerebral notes of logos are interspersed with the cries of the earth and the manifold emotions of the human soul. The rushing of rivers, the whispering of pines, the howling of wolves, the eerie hollow silences of canyons evoke the suffering of living beings. The short-lived harmony comes and goes. It is luxuriant and elusive.

An Indian ballad expresses the brooding and sorrowful longing of the songstress. The magnificent night has all but gone. Who knows when you will come. Loud shudderingly mournful and surreal wailings, rising to a high pitch like calls to prayer in the wee hours, as if there has been a death, are conveyed by wind instruments of East and West.

Ominous music conveys the conflict in Kurukshetra between form and feeling. The high octane atmosphere of intellect and strife and glory in high places is shattered by deep voices singing, *We Shall Walk through the Valley of the Shadow of Death* in the Ebenezer Baptist Church. The spirituals know all too well the slave ships and the dark shores and segregations of history. Nobody knows exodus and exile like they do. Nobody recites Elijah and sings of sweet chariots swinging low like the people of this church do. Nobody knows trouble like they do, and no one seeks justice, loves kindness, and walks humbly in community as they do.

The marchers in Birmingham chant "We Shall Overcome" even as the dogs and the police lines are in full view and the loudspeakers are heard. This sequence builds in volume and intensity until there is encounter and mayhem. A grave and enduring silence ensues, the marchers disperse, and in the distance is seen a mysterious messianic figure in the light of dusk. An avatar, a deity incarnate, or perhaps a phantom, he is a baritone approaching slowly with *Shall We Gather at the River*.

The person who will lead us will not lead us in a violent path that leads to abomination and death, but in a nonviolent one that leads to justice and peace. The shepherd will not lead the flock astray into aggression and harm's way. Lesser leaders lead the people into war, oppression, and a destructive alienation from nature. This one will have studied the past and will know the awesome burden of leadership. Sitar and tabla can blend well with piano and strings. East and West coexist throughout, as do the past and the future in the present. The music is harmonious here, a blending of heaven and earth, because our leader sees the wide picture and is thoughtful and wise and inclusive.

The abstract notes of reason clash and compromise again with the visceral music of love, longing, and protest. The lofty music of the gods recedes and rallies, alternating with the emotional, abdominal chords of contingent, gritty earth. Chords on both sides resist and bend. They give and take. This oscillation, this mutual information and molding between the requirements of the forms and the imperfections of the flesh, is polar and eternal. The blending and harmonization of the ideal and the actual are rare, occurring in times of great hope and love.

The polity of the denomination I served for a while was hierarchical and did not feel right for me. But I should have known, given the above music of opposite worlds, that the Unitarian Universalist denomination would not be the right match for me either. I joined and even preached in the big church in Atlanta for a while and came to know the pastor and the Council members.

To explore all my options was important, I thought, before I made the consequential yet delicate decision as to my affiliation. I remember the pastor in my new church preaching that life moves spirally upward. We start with our religion, move outward to be enriched by what the wider world offers, then return to our religious roots, only at a higher level. This process continues into the next cycle. Most sermons are forgotten and some sermons are remembered vaguely and in fragments. The contents of this sermon must have resonated like a church bell on Sunday morning, because they were unforgettable.

To propel my own sermon forward I used Socrates and his myth of the cave as illustrative material, and also the famous section from the *Chandogya Upanishad* about the pieces of salt being divided into smaller and smaller pieces until only the invisible essence remains.

The culture in that church, however, felt almost one-dimensional, nor did I form warm friendships there whose support and encouragement I seemed to need. It looked smoggy for me, like the skyline of Los Angeles from a distance at times, as I peered down the Universalist Unitarian road. While the worship had some intellectual heft, it did not strike the deeper and more intimate chords within. A wider frame of reference, whose cultures and religions and ethnicities are legion, is possibly what I needed. And it was important that I have a friendly and supportive community. This was true especially since I came in time to imagine an abstruse role for myself in the theater of existence, perhaps as a blind composer playing sidereal nocturnes for mountain villages deep in the night, or as a monk writing his secret diary of dark desires.

16

Atlanta

The person of heaven gives to the person of dust a prayer

THE DIVORCE BROKE MY heart. I covered the waterfront, but only to pace. A magical episode of my life had ended, the moon in the river, the forest's green darkness, the Judy Collins and Joan Baez and Billie Holliday songs in the soft red living room.

I had faced sadness before, as in the train knowing I would be left in a cold and snowy place far, far away. There was deep silence in the train's compartment, and the depth of that silence told me that my aunt's sadness was as dark as mine. My sadness now was layer upon layer of fresh memories, new projections of dreadful things that might happen to Mariah, and the guilt I would bear. I was staring into a void. There was nothing I could do but try to go on with my life and let her go on with hers.

I took Cuchulain and Mariah took Iona. The old terrier Sammy had died. I dreamed of Sammy recently. He got lost. I saw him go into the woods and I gave chase, fearing for his safety. But the woods were a hilly rubble of rocks, deep fissures among the rocks, and a jungle with tangled vines. I thought I saw him, but then I lost him again. It was a sad and frightening dream.

My personal life had been steadily sinking into moral disarray as Mariah and I had drifted further and further apart. The moon in the river and the forest's green darkness was how I exegeted the years of our marriage. The poem I wrote wallowed pathetically in depression, sentimentality, and the contortions that resulted from them. A female philosophy colleague did not like it.

I sought help first in group therapy. There was a low-cost program run out of the psychology department's graduate division in another university. Later I began seeing a psychiatrist, who immediately resisted the psychological categories in which I had entrenched myself. He told me, interestingly enough, that he had been influenced by a book by an existentialist psychiatrist. The big knowledge I thought I possessed turned out to be the little knowledge that is a dangerous thing. He was the skinny fox who grew suspicious of the one-way footprints into the lion's cave. What, then, was wrong with me?

The psychiatrist would play with his telephone cord, wrapping and unwrapping it around his wrist and hand and leaving it dangling in knots. He took an interest in the poetry I wrote and listened to lines I wrote at Stone Mountain. He sent *The Ashram of E. Stanley Jones* to a relative who was an English professor. She in turn wrote back a supportive letter suggesting gently that I needed to grow out of my Elioticism. It was true. I thrived in the shadow of "April is the cruellest month" and I heard the same dry sterile thunder without rain. I asked the same questions, Who is the third who walks beside you? Were we led all that way for Birth or for Death?

Eliot's broodingly minimalist language of fear and forsakenness were an exact fit in the valley of dry bones. Storied history and tragedy lurk in the desert along the border. Books and songs of lone mavericks, eccentric ramblers and rangers, tumbleweed roads leading anywhere and nowhere, and old empty shacks against sand, wind, and time strike some innate chord, stir some distant memory of vacant fields in the hot sun and buzzards on a dead, skinless tree. Aliens and strangers cross paths. High-flying eagles circle the sky for the remains of coyote and cougar kills. The cactus and thorn tree and gnarled juniper landscapes rattle and hiss and howl with danger. The sizzling music in the air is Mexican American desert songs of loneliness in a border town's tavern, sparse chants and refrains of longing and desolation and scarcity. A man on horseback approaches Hondo slowly and guardedly, trailed by dust. He remembers what happened here fifteen years ago when he was a boy.

I had written *The Ashram of E. Stanley Jones* a few years earlier. It was not the theology of Brother Stanley that I was remembering and retrieving, but the transcendence, the release from the emotional entanglements of the world. We were woken early by the bell, and we made our way to the round chapel in the pines. Leaving our shoes at the door, we sat on the floor with our Bibles in silence.

The legendary seventy-year-old writer and religious figure dressed in a white dhoti and kameez outfit sat crosslegged and looked through the dust particles in the first sunbeams. He had served as a Methodist missionary in India for fifty years, had met Gandhi and Nehru and other leaders in the Indian National Movement, had written scores of internationally acclaimed devotional books and held countless retreats and conferences and interreligious dialogues in the YMCAs and other venues across the land and in his Sat Tal ashram in the Himalayan foothills, where my college friends Mohit and Gilchrist and I now sat. Congress had just passed legislation in the mid-fifties disallowing missionaries, but he had been a friend of Indian independence and would be allowed to come and go as he pleased.

Toward the end of the early morning hour Brother Stanley's ruminations included affirming references to Gandhi on one occasion. People from all over India were present, a bearded and robed Bishop Alexander mar Theophilus from the Mar Thoma Church in South India, two young doctors in love from the Christian Medical College and hospital in Ludhiana, where my father had been pastor when I was in kindergarten, a European Sister Lila, and many others. Bishop Theophilus and some others followed Brother Stanley and shared their own inspirations during the silent time. At the close of the hour we lined up in twos and walked to breakfast singing *I Will Not Be Afraid*, a song written by a missionary in China.

Something about the songs and the togetherness and the message of the risen Christ walking beside us equipped us with music and memories and meanings for the vagaries of a rapidly changing world, which we would soon face. Gilchrist, Mohit, and I were at the cusp of our careers. Important decisions would soon be made as to what and where and when. Our future in the plains was unknown. This was precious food not just for missionaries and pilgrims on their vicissitudinous journeys, but for seekers after Truth everywhere, for aid workers reading Brother Stanley's books in faraway dangerous places, for young women and men striving for Goodness in their wilderness of trial and temptation.

E. Stanley Jones was the sunken treasure I pulled up from the ocean floor as I brooded upon the dark waters of my career choices. The ashram was a signal on the lines as I stood at the crossroads in Atlanta looking up and down, waiting for a train to pass. It was just at that juncture that I met the Reverend Bill Scott Jr., pastor of one of the United Church of Christ congregations in that city. Bill and the worship and setting of the church, the warm embrace of the people, and the denomination itself felt right. The front wall was all glass, revealing pines. I had worked in Highland and Pasadena with United Church of Christ congregations and thus felt that I knew this place.

Bill was a reserved dark-haired middle-aged man with dignity in his manner and just a trace of mischief in the way he talked. It was not that he invited or encouraged me to settle and seek ministry in this denomination. There was acknowledgement, yes, but there was also a sort of coolness, a demurring, a contradiction about him that I could not comprehend, nor did I try. At one point he said, The Presbyterians owe you. He was referring to my San Anselmo experience, I knew, but I wondered what he meant. There was more to him than met the eye, and it was not forthcoming.

Nonetheless, his sermons and prayers and his conduct of worship were at once cool and electrifying. This was the first time I had experienced such compelling worship, though I had heard great preachers before, like Billy Graham in New Delhi and San Anselmo, E. Stanley Jones in the Himalayas, Norman Vincent Peale on the high seas on the way to Honolulu. Bill was uniquely gifted. He said things obliquely and poetically. At one point he quoted Charles Peguy's *Mystery of the Holy Innocents* at length. Airy, transparent, and even playful, his sermons did not elicit attention to themselves. Instead, they disarmed you and made you say, This at last has got to be true. Look, he's so deft with words, he's having such a good time in the pulpit, and he's making sense too. Look, he's talking about last week's television shows about cops and robbers, about the good guys and bad guys. The sermons and prayers drew you in unknowingly and carried you away. But I had the sense that no one in the congregation appreciated Bill as much as I did.

Bill appeared to be a plain, unpretentious man with a turn of phrase who seemed unaware of just how talented he was. His sermons did not wear their truth on their sleeve. They forced no linear argument or correct conclusion on the mind, no faux intensity on the soul. They were the work of an extraordinary mind. There were those who would rather hear linear arguments leading to correct conclusions. They found the sermons wanting.

It was important for me that I feel free in my religion, and more than that, I knew I needed a role model that rose above the mediocre. Bill's presence in the pulpit was what I would look to for many years hence. Truth is in the letting be. Truth is in the call forward, deeply heard in the bones. Truth is in the purity of heart. Truth is in the aesthetic, the melody and tone, the singing.

The sermons, however, were still evangelical in the good sense. Their language steeped in the Christian texts, of which they took full advantage, they just knew that everyone is a crook, that there is only one keeper of promises, that bishops and priests and ministers can be bought off for small change, and that the person of heaven gives to the person of dust the gift of a lifetime, a prayer, the latter not having a prayer in the world.

Religion and poetry went well together in Bill's hands. George Santayana had famously said that when religion merely supervenes upon life it is poetry, but when poetry intervenes in life it is religion. Bill exploited the language of the Christian texts to weave his poetry, and when he delivered those words in worship they became religion for us. Word advened in the world, logos cleaved the sky and cohorted with life, essence descended with grace and truth and engaged existence. Theologians call this immanence, a formal word in theology which means the presence of transcendence in the world. Thus the name Emmanuel, from the same root, means God with us.

Bill himself was of a piece with his poetry. He was quick and funny. During coffee hour he stood with Mary in one place, and you had to go to him if you wanted to talk to him. Were there places he faltered? He hid them layers and layers beneath his public persona. You had to peer deeply, pay close attention, read between the lines, and even then you were wrong.

As a token of my admiration of him, and aware of his love for words, I brought him my spare copy of Austin's *Sense and Sensibilia*. Observing him be himself so easily in the pulpit, I knew that I could aspire to be myself too. No being buried alive anymore, half of me, in the ground.

17

Stone Mountain

There's a fire softly burning, supper's on the stove

A SMALL CHURCH JUST off the seacoast of Maine, north of Bar Harbor, called me to be their pastor after an exchange of handwritten letters. Just the idea of the sea and a lighthouse broke all my chains. Of course I said yes. I would never look back. I would not regret turning down another offer that came from Florida. I would thrive in the arms of this small community of church persons by the river. It would be my escape from the lying eyes of the city. The salt winds would summon me to the sea, I would hold time in my hands, and I would be a poet and a muse.

The offer came just before my ordination when I was serving out a year as a chaplain intern in a downtown hospital. It was actually useful supervised training for the pastorate. We brought in detailed verbatims of our visits on the floors, scripts which were photocopied and distributed to our colleagues and supervisors and submitted to excruciating analysis. I overheard one of our supervisors use the word "existentia" in the corridor.

Relativity ruled my brand new world. The chaplains sneered like Pilate, What is truth? and then added, What is your truth? They meant it too. There was no philosophizing with these guys. They would mock you, hand you to the mob to be crucified if you claimed some purchase on royalty. But they gave you religious freedom. They did not expect you to say things you did not believe. I treasured this. First there was Bill, whose gifts soared high above mediocrity. Now there were these tough-minded, brave-hearted, deep-thinking chaplains. What the cultured despisers of religion do not know is that religion need not be for the feebleminded, and it need not be authoritarian.

This time it was philosophy that I would suspend for a year, or perhaps forever. Plato to Wittgenstein would now be my buried treasure as I entered this labyrinth of midnight shifts, emergency room death calls, burn unit and intensive care unit and morgue visits, and having to deal with nurses and doctors, and to write all of this up in the wee hours of the morning.

One young professional woman was very pretty and flirtatious, a playful and very bright princess in a Moghul palace. Her hair was as black as midnight and she had big, brown all-knowing eyes. She knew that the sky is blue, that the world is round, and that the wind is high. There was no place to hide.

There was meaning in this work. My transition continued into the immanent domain of mediating the logos of hope and grace and love in the land of despair and guilt and trauma. In this realm the chaplain counsels and consoles at bedside above the sirens of perpetual perishing, the enlightened philosopher returns to take his seat in the cave of shadows, and the bodhisattva serves with compassion in the back streets and alleys of suffering beings. Whether they are human or nonhuman who feed at the garbage dumps there, it does not matter. Here in Kurukshetra, amid the dust and rumble of chariots, the person of heaven gives to the person of dust a prayer.

Last night I dreamed I was in a circus, and a lion escaped from its cage and was loose. Everyone was in a panic. I hid in the trailer until the lion was captured and placed in its cell. So someone said in a crowded seminar room of interns and seminary students. That, mused the balding supervisor, who had a PhD from the University of Chicago Divinity School, is liberal theology. Meaning that Lust and Wrath can be curbed, and we can regard this world once more as our home.

Someone else then expressed the horrifying thought that the lion was still loose, everyone had panicked, you had hid in the trailer, but the lion was in that very trailer. That, reflected the supervisor with a gleam in his eye, is conservative theology. We are in the world but not of the world. We are aliens, threatened and unhappy in this life, as Kierkegaard had said, in which Lust and Wrath are relentless and rampant.

There was truth, I thought, in both those theologies. That the lion was back safe in its cell was confirmed by my being now on the way to ordination and a vocation that finally felt right for me, and by my call to ministry in a faraway lighthouse landscape where the tide swells the river, the waves wash the seaweeds on the craggy shore, and the blue winds sweep clean the boulders and the beaches. That the lion was still on the loose was mirrored in my dissolute entrances through doors marked Nevermore, and my having fallen madly for that young woman at the hospital, a hapless condition I dared not reveal to anyone. I had always fallen madly in love, and I would always fall madly in love.

I dreamed up my own theological project to draw the two points of view together into some sort of montage. Dr. Zero, alias the Rev. Dr. Theo, returning to his underground lab of experimental potions and serums, alloys of naturalism and Platonism and existentialism and on and on, would soldier his way beyond both neo-orthodox existentialist type theologies and liberal philosophical type theologies and become famous for discovering the hidden interface between the two paradigms, a prize coveted by theologians East and West. He would be the one that would build a dialectical bridge between the philosophical and theological shores.

Finally to penetrate the uncontrollable mystery on the bestial floor and bring to light the true meaning of these days would be the task of Dr. Zero. He would answer the question about God and thus solve the conundrum of the Eternal and Universal Thou, whether it was an abstract Platonic entity of which the particular Thous were instances, one of the ultimate particles or forces of which the universe is composed, or something else of a different nature entirely. He would bring intellect and depth and extraordinary preaching skills to the pulpit. His fame would spread far and wide and he would become senior pastor of the prestigious Riverside Church in New York City.

Life in the big utilitarian city can deplete us emotionally. Someone asks if something is wrong, but they themselves are too burned to wait for an answer. They move quickly on to some other tasks. A phase of your life has ended, the grueling phase of a divorce or of searching for suitable work. Now you know that your new start by the sea is a sheer gift. I was eager to leave.

In the meantime you flee for solitude and silence to brood in a secret refuge closer by, a place with trees and brooks and rocks that hold you close and heal you. At the foot of Stone Mountain were nature trails with streams, chestnut and tulip and umbrella trees, hollies and rhododendrons, the thrush's warble and the blue jay's shrill cry, all manner of living things for the healing of the nations. The forest floor was a carpet of rich black soil upon which shafts of sunlight projected shifting patterns. The monumental granite slabs of the mountain rose steeply, and scattered clusters of pine here and there offered shade for hikers in the summer. The lostness here was a good lostness, as in I and Thou, in which the I separately and the Thou separately are both lost in the encounter.

In the last days, while filing out of church on Sunday morning, I picked up a copy of the speech said to be delivered by Chief Seattle before the signing of the 1855 Treaty of Point Eliot. That church had given me so much, the pulpit example of Bill Scott, my ordination, the knowledge of the order and aesthetic and aura of worship, trustworthy church friends who gave me warm clothes to take with me to Maine, and now this poignant lamentation on the loss of one's land.

The authenticity of the speech is in doubt, but it reads like a magnificent requiem for the earth and all its creatures. Every valley and hillside is sacred, and the soil can respond lovingly to our footsteps if we but walk softly. Sad-voiced winds moan in the distance. When the braves return from the beyond in the mist of the imagination to console and comfort, will they indeed ever find the eagle-flown plains and verdant windswept valleys, the groves and rocks and thickets and somber solitudes? Or will these have surrendered to the White Man's plough and pollution and plunder? The Red Man runs from the White Man, and wherever the Red Man goes he hears the footsteps of his White destroyer, just as the wounded doe hears the approach of the hunter.

Years later I would read this speech as a sermon on an Independence Day Sunday, which I called America Sunday, to a teary-eyed Taiwanese-backgrounded congregation. I now think that perhaps I should not have done so.

Truth in the big sense was contained in the stapled papers I carefully tucked among my most important books and documents, which I packed into my compact car, along with my warm clothes. It was Truth in the big sense because the speech was so transparent of sacred ground. Cuchulain would stay in a kennels, and I arranged with a friend to ship him up when I was settled. The radio played *Lying Eyes* and a John Denver song about going back home again as I drove north. Every year as a boy I would go home. I still weep when I hear that John Denver song. Now I was going home again.

It was Christmas Eve I remember.

18

The Narraguagus

*I eat of the Tree of the Knowledge
of Good and Evil*

Color the new chapter of my life a sixty-acre wooded estate of old-growth hemlocks with nests in the summer of eagles and ospreys plunging into the Narraguagus River for salmon and of snow owls hooting at night. This was in Down East Maine, ingressed by the sea. My church and the estate, which was owned by the Maine Seacoast Missionary Society, both overlooked the river. The big parsonage was located in the estate. I knew in the marrow of my bones even then that I had to be one of the luckiest pastors alive.

The river was turning to ice when I arrived, and it began to snow. Deeper and deeper got the snow, and it became impossible to walk to church through the woods on the forgotten dirt road with its ditches and fallen logs and old cedars, especially in the dark on Thursdays for choir practice. What pack of wolves prowls in the night? Is it a bear that can do me harm? Or is it just the wind stirring the branches that I hear?

No, too often I braved the slush and the white wind and the blowing and drifting snow on Route 1 instead, where there were lights from passing cars and the retirement apartments and Tracy's Motel. There were Thursdays when I drove to Tommy and Gladys's overlooking the river on the other side. First of the day, they would say in a sing-song voice, lifting their glasses. This was followed by peanuts to mask the smell before the rehearsal. Tommy was the one who I had corresponded with. He had met

The Narraguagus

Gladys at Macy's in Boston a long, long time ago. The conversation would return to this most times I visited.

Trying to preach in an oblique style using soft light brush strokes as I had intended turned out to be unnatural for me. My sermons would not lead, however, to a formulaic way of pronouncing shibboleth. I had learned enough from Bill Scott, nonethelsss, to keep them airy and lively, though rooted in the Biblical texts, and the people warmed up to them. In time I was a hit. I remember preaching on the burning bush. I probably mused on our own religious grounds-zero, sacred places hallowed by some unquenchable fire, out of which our own names are called. There was a ground zero everywhere you looked, up and down the river, on the blueberry ridge, beside the sea.

The young parents brought the youth to the parsonage. Several elderly stalwarts of the church attended my weekly Bible discussion group in the living room of the parsonage. Tommy and Gladys came, along with Edith and Arthur, Ed and Barbara, the powerful clerk of the church Charlotte Tucker, and others. A youngish and attractive brown-eyed, brown-haired woman who co-owned a pizza place with her partner in an adjoining town attended occasionally. I had met her there when I stopped for a snack, which I did often on my way to Machias for regional meetings.

I had had Cuchulain flown up to the Bangor airport as soon as I arrived in Down East Maine. He had meowed at the top of his lungs when he heard my voice at the claims counter. In the big house my only companion explored the basement with its large furnace and checked out the bedrooms upstairs, where he and I would listen to the hooting of owls at night.

A denominational leader came to preach at my small church. On my request he had written a letter to the church about Gay rights. He had admonished the people in the letter to look at the subject from historical, ethical, pastoral, and theological perspectives, but the church people in that small town of three thousand did not even know what these terms meant. We spent time on Saturday night talking about theology and America. He shared with me our church's plans for President Jimmy Carter's upcoming visit to Maine. I liked this man and the intelligent and courageous way he spoke about the politics of our times.

Spring came and the countryside, stirring with life, metamorphosed into apple blossoms and wild flowers and grasses. I was happy and wrote a poem about the skinless trees along the coast before they died, and how in the morning I would show you the town and the river, the salmon against time and the river, against eagle and osprey, against the crain that darkens the world upon changing to another rock. The other day a skinny fox, on reaching the river and putting up its nose to smell, swam across to farmyards. In the old wooden chapel close to the parsonage a bee fell silent when I was writing, and the silence was noisier than the humming. And my church on the river saying, Come from the east and the west, from the north and the south. Come for the joyful feast of the children of God. Come, those who stay here and those who visit and those who pass by. Come away from the truth of the silence in the chapel, come away from the truth of the skinny fox, come away from the truth of the waiting birds.

Occasionally I drove to Boston for an overnight stay, but after church on Sundays I was usually off pell-mell to Bar Harbor an hour to the south. Being the gateway to Acadia National Park, it was crowded with tourists and had a busy marketplace where I found a cafe with a diner ambience and scrumptious local blueberry pie. Then off to the Park with its panorama of cliffs and the crashing of the Atlantic waves upon the boulders.

But I was alone among the clamor of cormorants and on the trails around lakes and the quiet old Rockefeller carriage roads with their stone bridges overhead. The sighing of the wind, the murmuring of the stream, and the thickets of cedars and birches and berry shrubs on Mount Cadillac made this place as blissful as the nature trails of Stone Mountain and as the soft clay slope and secret rhododendron tree of my boyhood. Groundedness and solitude mix, however, with the craving for someone to love. Ecstacy and inquietude are soulmates in Kurukshetra. The coolness and the balm of Infinite Goodness are breathed through the heat of desire.

David Tracy's *The Blessed Rage for Order* came at just the right time. I devoured the eloquent neo-Catholic theologian's new book in my woodsy home from cover to cover. His was a voice as fresh as a mountain spring. What drew me in was that his passion for both philosophy and theology coincided with my own. In that way he was also of the same ilk as Paul Tillich and John Cobb Jr. It was Tracy's stated aim, furthermore, to show how Christian faith and identity could be understood to cohere with a perfectly secular philosophical sensibility.

It was clear from the start, partly because of the pompousness of such a claim, that his project was doomed to failure. Yet I loved the sheer energy and skill and even flamboyance with which it was being iterated and elaborated. The pages bristled with the postmodern spiritual quandary in extravagant perspicacious detail, and his definition of authenticity as allowing oneself openness to the infinitely expanding horizon had the sound of chains breaking and ancient prison doors banging open. When I quoted that definition in my sermons I had the small congregation by the river in the palm of my hand. Listening to the jingle-jangle pandemonium of pluralism and the clanging cymbals of contemporaneity conjured up on every page, I cheered him on as he approached his final ascent to the Mount St. Anselm summit, sublimely oblivious of the weight of his grandiloquence and panache.

It was mainly Tracy's neoclassical philosophical baggage that I blamed for his failure, but it really did not matter. Tracy was just the right author to reignite my theological soul, and it was then that I myself began to write. The lion loose and the lion captured was a vivid dichotomy to use, and I framed my project then in terms of stages, a first conservative stage, a second more mature liberal stage, and I thought I had a third stage that would be a sort of mystical mélange of the two earlier stages with the focus on spirit. This third stage, however, turned out to be ill-defined and ill-advised, as would become clearer to me later. It obscured the view of the rapids and falls coming right up.

I was not really ready to write, just perhaps to make notes, and I was distracted. The solitude of this home in the woods was deepening and closing in around me like prison walls. The marketplace in Bar Harbor, the rocky cliffs by the sea, and the entertainments of Boston were beckoning like lights on a yonder shore.

Pilgrim, in Paradise the two opposing Pauline laws of good and evil working in our members is the palpable germ of the story, though we must be careful to distinguish this war from the gulf between intellect and existence, between metaphysics and history, or between spirit and flesh, both sides of which can harbor evil and be fertile ground for good. The former of these pairs can be a place of domination or of wisdom and the latter of gluttony or love.

I was not prepared for the Pauline war. It came upon me unexpectedly, like an earthquake. The Woman and I went to the Tree of the Knowledge of Good and Evil at the center of the Garden, and the Serpent, disguised now as Love, cast a spell upon me and struck, and I ate of the Tree's fruit. Just then I knew that I had ruined my first pastoral opportunity and the Paradise I had been given.

Immediately intense *maya* enveloped the garden, a foggy surreal haze in which nothing looked as it really was. I could feel the poison sinking into the cells and interstices of my soul and the numbness growing. I could not with Augustine use youthfulness as an excuse, for I was no longer a youth, nor did the chaste dignity of continence allure me with her imagined multitude of chaste young men and maidens. The thick veil of ignorance blinded me to the consequences of my actions. Perspicuous only were guilt and the competition of the two laws for power. When God walked in the evening I hid among the balsam. A voice called my name from beyond the trees, but the voice close behind me was the cold hiss of glass-eyed Death.

It pains me to write about the mendacity and wantonness of my own actions. Would that I could expunge this episode from my past and from my mind. To omit it from my story, however, would be to convey an untrue picture to my pilgrim readers. To keep it up front, if only in my own soul, is for me to remember that first place of ordained ministry as sacred. It came with an unquenchable and unconsuming fire. The lesson I learned here would be my guide and stay for the rest of my life. What fools we are when we do not learn from our mistakes. It is they who tell us who we are and what we are capable of and incapable of.

These things must be told, that I violated my own sense of moral decency, that I gave away my power yet again, that I had no strength left, and no ground but sinking sand left to stand on, and that the four walls of fear were closing in around me. I was desperate to escape, but each option I may have had was no match for the deficiencies in my own character. I was entangled and much too fragile to regain control. Death had begun to stalk me.

I have no music, no poem for you now, Pilgrim, only what the prophet cries. The grass withers, the flower fades, the summer comes to an end. Things add up, says John Cobb. The place was new and fresh and clean, the people served pure homemade butter at Thanksgiving, the older women and men had their own peculiar way of saying yes. They said *aya*. Beautiful bohemian youth from the outside with torn jeans and green philosophies and Gaia hypotheses espoused natural and local foods and built their own houses. Fireflies signaled bioluminescently in the indigo dark and the firmament declared its knowledge by starlight upon the dirt path. The pebbles were smooth upon the beaches, the ponds serene, the waves crashed loud against the rocks, the trails soft and colorful and fragrant with pine, the sky big and busy with flocks of sea birds flying north and south between the islands. But I was the same person of dust, an unfathomably broken vessel, and historically ill-prepared for the solitudinous splendor I had been given.

The Narraguagus

Shorn of my academic mask I am naked in the Garden. My knowledge stands revealed as the little knowledge that is a dangerous thing, and pure reason offers no life support in a stormy sea. The disconnect between our embrace of lofty principles of thought and a contingent wave-tossed existence like a ship at sea has troubled this book from the start. This is the generic divide we have alluded to often, both levels of which can be arenas in which good and evil thrive.

On the higher level I was thankful for the consolation of Paul and Augustine and Kierkegaard, with their liberations and lections and leaps, and for the exhortation of Buber and Niebuhr, with their empathy for the human quandary. In this remote morass of Lust and Jealousy and Wrath, however, I needed a companion, a counselor, a comforter in the flesh, and I knew of no such person here. I would have to learn on my own the conditions, within and without, that spawn shameful actions. My own sins would have to teach me that actions have consequences, and that we cannot undo our actions. The lion was loose.

19

The Berkshires

Deception and truth walked hand in hand on the village green

I FLED FROM THE Garden. But the new church's location in the Berkshires was also Paradise, with its own picturesque New England village, its hills and hemlocks and winding country roads, the historic covered bridge over the river, the Appalachian Trail and nature preserves, the river and streams and waterfalls, and the field where the cow jumped over the moon. That overgrazed field was at the back of the parsonage.

My mother and father came from India for the wedding. I had been glad for many years that they were now living together in Ludhiana, where my father had become pastor again of his old church, the church in the big mission compound where I went to kindergarten and wrote in Urdu on a slate. The church still serves, among others, the staff of the Christian hospital and medical college there. This would be the last time I would see my mother. She would die a few years later of complications resulting from diabetes. To this day I keep enlarged separately taken photographs of my parents on that occasion prominently displayed in my living room.

I had actually planned to extricate myself from my entanglement in Down East Maine, but I learned the hard way that there are things you cannot run away from. The officiating pastor was the Reverend Raymond Hahn, who came down from Bar Harbor. He was innocent of my information, he was humble and warm, he was moderate in his theology. After the service the congregation followed the bagpipes to the large house which

The Berkshires

belonged to Polly and Frank, longtime environmentally wealthy church members who had donated some of their hillside land behind their house to The Nature Conservancy. Softspoken Frank would spend time splitting logs, and outspoken Polly would dash madly to the post office and around town in her red Volkswagen bug beeping like Road Runner oblivious of the scheming Coyote in the cartoons.

I had come to love the Woman and to understand her, which was not easy. She looked twice as pretty with her wedding dress and windy bouquet of wildflowers prepared by an exquisitely elegant older church woman originally from New York City. My bride's smile managed to beam lovelight but throw a shadow at the same time. Both ends of her lips appeared sometimes to curve downward ever so slightly. I asked myself subconsciously what that meant. Did it connote self-doubt? Was it a built-in sense of the tragic? And did these meanings play a role in the allure she had over me? I will not speculate about these things here and risk casting aspersions that I do not intend. Serious personal constraints dogged each of us, I knew, but I will confine myself to my own story, which I believe I can tell with some effectiveness, if not completeness, without trespassing into hers.

Niebuhr speaks endlessly of the baffling confusion of nature and spirit in human experience, of sin and creation in the same act, of the admixture of self-seeking and virtue in the dramas of history. This was the day when deception and truth walked hand in hand on the village green, betrayal and beauty danced cheek to cheek in the crowded old New England house, and the people raised their glasses.

My father told a wedding joke. The couple being married were sent a congratulatory telegram, which read just "1 John 4: 18," which says in part that there is no fear in love, but perfect love casts out fear. But in the process of transmittal the "1" in "1 John" had gotten deleted, and the telegram on arrival read "John 4:18," which says that you have had five husbands, and the one you now have is not your husband. The people laughed.

But it was no laughing matter. No one there knew what had taken place to bring this union about. The consequences blew against me like the north wind. Death hung around the parsonage like a monsoon mist. It seeped in through the walls, dampening them and the furniture and the bed sheets. Hollow primeval wails of dread and foreboding could be heard in Kurukshetra. Sin's venom was working. The Cobra with its dagger eyes rose portentiously to the snake-charmer's reed from the bag. The hypnotic nasal bamboo sound echoed in the village and in the hills, and the Cobra danced, its body coiling in the air and head moving from side to side.

I must have known at some level that the people could see me discombobulate. My sermons got theatrical and egoistic. They spoke of apple blossoms and hummingbirds, charming the congregation with poetry. Or else they were accusatory and invidious, foisting liberal political guilt on conservative people. I could see the look of disbelief and sometimes anger on some of their faces. And the cobra danced.

You do not understand us, Frank told me as gently as he could in a meeting of our Executive Committee. Another man who took home tapes of my sermons for his invalid wife said that my sermons seemed disjointed. He had had time to parse them. A woman hinted that my pastoring was overwrought. How much did the congregation pick up as they saw my ministry and my marriage unfold before their eyes? Was I really driven by my demons? Were my pastoral visits a way to hide my guilt? Were my sermonic excesses a rouge to camouflage my deficiencies, or perhaps my depression? My ministry was not going well, and everyone knew I had relinquished my power.

I found Cuchulain dead outside. I took his body in a plastic bag into the hills and left it in the trees. I do not know how he died.

One bright spot in my bleak winter was Archie Jamgotchian. A slight, olive-skinned man with glasses and a serious air, he would come to my office to talk with me about the liturgical seasons, his Orthodox background, and especially the welfare of animals. Instinctively I joined him in his expressions of solidarity with the nonhuman creation, and he took me to a state hearing on the leg-hold trap. I remember the young pretty state senator saying about one leg-hold trap defender's demonstration that he hadn't completed it. She was waiting for him to bite off his arm.

Archie led me deeper into the world of compassion and activism, and a whole world I had not known unfolded before my eyes. He had his own nonprofit organization, to whose board meetings I sat in on two or three times. He and I in fact paved the way for our regional church conference to adopt a resolution that year affirming the church's concern for all creation. Thank you, Archie, for your quiet but persistent advocacy for those who cannot speak for themselves. You were quietly determined and single-minded in your labors, and I held you and hold you still close to my heart. I heard of your death many years later through your church's newsletter, and I was sad. You did not know, nor did I at the time, how much I was learning from you, and how much of a lifeline you were for me, like the River Niger is said to be for a wooded savanna in West Africa. It sustains a multitude of plant and mammal species.

This was a bigger and wealthier church than the one in Maine. The people were educated, opinionated, and proud. A wealthy woman had swayed four or five church members to gather on Monday mornings to listen on tape to what struck me as the sermonic foppery of some pastor in a well-to-do church she called charismatic. I say this, however, partly out of sheer frustration. The actual contents of the tapes were not as miserable as the story of my own life. I refer here to my personal disconnect from my own sense of right and good, and to my anger at the brackish waters I had brought myself into. Both Kierkegaard and Takeuchi allude to philosophers who build magnificent palaces of thought but live a wretched existence in a small decrepit cottage.

Though weakened from the venom, I was staying alive. For much of the time I just took Death's blows, like Trevor when he went up against Milne from one of our opposing schools. Milne was the well-known star athlete not only of Saint George's itself but of the Mussoorie boarding schools generally. He was versatile, good in hockey, soccer, and track and field. In boxing the supple young man was pure science, pure poetry. Gliding around the ring, he was quick, agile, accurate. Trevor of our smaller school was thin and tall, bony, not strong. He was a fair-skinned Anglo-Indian, while Milne was a brown Anglo with a crewcut. At the interschool boxing tournament Trevor's face was red from the three rounds of punishment he had received. He had just been target practice for Milne, but he hadn't gone down. At the end of the year our principal Mr. Biggs justly awarded him the Best Loser Award. We all knew he deserved it and were proud of him when he walked up.

There was a level, however, at which I fought back, much like Lawie when he was in the ring with Pantha, this time in the intraschool tournament. The temperamental, explosive Pantha was a senior and had the upper hand, but Lawie was a brawler even when he was against the ropes. I knew that I was in the ring with Death itself, and that I had to find a way to muddle through this thing if I was going to survive.

Somewhere along the journey the road had broadened, and the extra lanes had made me complacent, wayward, even insolent in my ways, which in turn had resulted in careless love and the squandering of time, talent, and treasure. No moral and spiritual safeguards, imperatives, or disciplines kept me grounded. I did go to see a pastoral counselor in the city for help, but the city was far away and I dropped off. The task before me would use all my resources, even those that had not come into play before. The challenge was somehow to manage this quagmire of self-love and self-loathing, to learn to outmaneuver my Saboteur, to lie in wait, to steel and to shield myself, to bide my time.

It was turning out to be the biggest lesson of my life, and it had begun to manifest the fullness of its wrath. For years I would look back at this wedding inquisitive of its freight of meaning. What a beautiful and hallowed thing it all was, the kind unknowing pastor who came down from Bar Harbor with his wife, the wild flower bouquet and the pretty older woman who had crafted it, the bagpipes on the village green, the luxuriant pine environment where I climbed the Appalachian Trail, the presence of my mother and father, the big old house after the service, Polly and Frank, Peter Matthiessen's *The Snow Leopard*, which had just been published and which Polly had snapped up for me as soon as she saw it. That book was easy for me to devour because the scenery was so much like Landour. It is about Matthiessen's trip from Kathmandu deep into the Himalayas to see Shey Gompa, an ancient Buddhist shrine on Crystal Mountain in the land of Dolpo, and it won the National Book Award that year. It would all go down so uncommonly fraught with significance for me.

For now I was alone, and there was no place to run and hide. The denominational leader who had come to preach at my church in Maine and had been so collegial in my dealings with him was now acidic toward me. He knew everything.

20

Gotham City
I'll come running to see you again

The Saboteur won the early rounds. I had to upgrade my profile and seek another church, and soon two persons from the search committee of a New York City area church came to hear me preach. I happened to be in my element that day. The drama and gravitas with which I could read the drip, drop, drop, drop sequence from *The Wasteland*, conjuring a spring and a pool among the rocks and a hermit thrush among the pines as part of my sermon must have made an impression. Those lines were written for me. My empathy with Eliot was a gift I brought for the visitors, though it was also a dead give-away of my own dark side. They might have viewed this person as promising a thirsty church living water. Both their senior and assistant pastors had resigned. They did have an interim senior pastor, and they needed an assistant pastor to see them through the moonscape that lay ahead.

Be patient, I said to myself in the new environment, and forbear. Brood daily behind the bars of your mistakes. Adjust, learn all you can, and wait. Persevere and reshape yourself as best you can. You have to do what you have to do, said the brilliant family therapist. Then I thought, The time will come when all will be well. One day you will be grateful and know the secret of sorrow and existence.

Things did not go well in the new church either. The interim and I all but clashed. He did not like or trust me. Furthermore, this was a hugely talented and prosperous congregation with a Unitarian and secularist big city drift, and here I was after the interim left attempting prophetic sermons using lectionary themes and Biblical images. They were not well-received by some of the movers and shakers of that church.

I was miscast and dysfunctional in that youth group too, and felt unneeded for the vibrational theatrical productions that the adult advisors of the fifty or sixty youth were committed to doing. I did sing *You've Got a Friend* with the group in the closing gathering, and I learned a lovely new song, *Teach Your Children Well*. After the male-female effervescence of the rehearsals, those songs were able to create a tranquil if ephemeral circle of tenderness and tears.

In this church, however, there was a river of hope. In fact two rivers came together, like the Tigris and the Euphrates, to provide me sustenance in the Babylonian desert wilderness. One river was the few in the congregation who understood my sermons and responded to them enthusiastically. We agreed to participate in the Resurrection House soup kitchen in Harlem by preparing and serving food for the homeless and indigent. I helped cook *dal* with potatoes, cauliflower, onions, freshly chopped ginger and garlic, cumin, turmeric, and other sundry ingredients. It was a hit, and we all sat down at the same table to eat. In sharp contrast with my church, I felt as if I fit here with the people off the street and the few staff and volunteers. Here there was laughter and good humor and plain fun all around. In this soup kitchen, unlike in other similar places later, I could offer to say a prayer for the people before we ate, and the people would say Yeah, Yeah, Yeah in deep gravelly voices.

Lasting friendships were formed through this ministry, and it won me some favor both within myself and without. My activism in our regional anti-hunger network took me into Gotham City frequently, though sometimes I went into the city by myself and for myself at night.

The other river was the appearance of *The Liberation of Life* by Charles Birch and John Cobb, Jr. It was actually a pivotal theological event for me personally, and it again stimulated my own writing. In my woodsy parsonage in Down East Maine I had already started a manuscript in response to David Tracy's book, and now the church let me do a study leave in Claremont to pursue work on it under Cobb, who had been nothing but encouraging of me and generous with his time. Now he charged me nothing for writing under his guidance. It was during that study leave that I became acquainted with him on a personal level and even felt comfortable calling him by his first name.

The new book's chapter "Faith in Life" advocates an understanding of God as Life, which in turn is described as Creative Power, in the tradition of the process philosophers Charles Hartshorne and Alfred North Whitehead. This chapter is perhaps the clearest and best articulation I know about the theological sea change, the paradigm shift with which process theology is widely associated, and its leading idea made such intuitive sense to me. It was this idea that I had held in abeyance for later consideration when I read Henri Bergson on creative evolution and Cobb's *God and the World* as a student in Claremont. I could appreciate neither the idea's simplicity nor its manifold ramifications when I was younger. One after another I had postponed the weighty theological decisions for later, when it would be necessary to make them. That time was arriving, like a train coming around the bend, the crowded platform abuzz with anticipation.

The big questions about the concept of God, good and evil, the uncontrollable mystery on the bestial floor, the Eternal and Universal Thou, and the meaning of life itself had always been propulsive of my life journey. Now they were all arriving on the train together. I was about to join them and sit with them face to face, and they would demand all my attention. And even though I was still wanting to mysticize my responses, at least I knew I would be moving in the right direction.

When Birch and Cobb refer to Life, they are not meaning the abstract Platonic concept of Life. What could they be meaning but beings living in community in all their splendor and squalor, their cheetah and gazelle predaceous pursuits, their male and female carryings on? What entity can be an embodiment or instance of that abstract form other than these beings in their process of struggle and growth, of living and dying? Life the Creative Process indeed occurs manifestly in the plants, animals, people, and the plethora of living creatures all around us.

The chapter "Faith in Life" refers us helpfully to Henry Nelson Wieman's distinction between created goods and the Creative Good. Created goods are perceptible, measurable, individual things of someone's making or doing, like this pen with which I am writing. Computers and cathedrals and catalogues are created goods. They have no life of their own. The Creative Good, by contrast, is the busy, ingenious hands and minds that created those things. The difference between created goods and the Creative Good is the difference between things that moth and rust corrupt and things that neither moth nor rust can corrupt, living things that as male and female and in community with others procreate their own dynamic, self-generative kind and thus endure from generation to generation.

The mystery of the Creative Good is the mystery of the ocean of Life itself. It is the complex incorporeal brew by which our lives adapt, adjust, and move forward in the face of danger, oppression, boredom, loneliness, disease, or some unforeseen circumstance or limiting condition.

Desire arises, and passion, as Sartre knew during the German occupation. Because of it we were never more free, he said famously. And those of us who knew the secrets asked ourselves, If they torture me, will I betray my comrades? Then we were face to face with the most basic question of who we are, the question of freedom. Or as William James knew when, in the face of his own mental and physical ailments and the total push and pressure of the cosmos, he sprang to life upon reading an essay of Renouvier and upon choosing to believe in his own free will and creative power. Or as Gandhi and Martin Luther King Jr. and Mandela knew when, in the face of a thousand slights, a thousand indignities, their passion grew and they were drawn into the political fray.

But how to channel our desire, our drive? We brood upon the waters. We imagine the possibilities, ideas come and go, and we chose to arise and go to our own lake isle of Inisfree. Perhaps it is stress or sadness that points us there to build our cabin of clay and wattles and live alone in the bee-loud glade. The realization that we must go there, where peace comes dropping slow, galvanizes us to action.

A million myriad ingredients, of course, may go in various combinations into the unseen brew of the Creative Good, ideas, intelligence, imagination, memory, craftsmanship, ingenuity, instinct, intuition, wisdom, energy, empathy, ability to collaborate with others, conviction, courage, inspiration, determination, the ability to incorporate new experience into one's own sense of self, the capacity for pleasure, the will to live, playfulness, good humor. The disequilibrium of form and feeling, philosophy and poetry, metaphysics and music, male and female, East and West, and North and South fuels and guides the Creative Process moment by moment to its yonder shore. Life oscillates like church bells in the evening, spirals like the whirlwind at noon. Both poles of the oppositions have their turn. Or else, lacking balance, the Process goes awry.

Armed with such a complex and rich understanding, it makes intuitive sense to affirm the mystery of the biodiverse Creative Process as sacred and trustworthy, and to take the natural, unforced step of saying to it, God.

Created goods are like grass that withers and flowers that fade, to echo the prophet. Even individual people are grass. But the Creative Good, which is Creative Power in the most general sense, is forever. In this sense, Creative Process does not occur in human beings alone but in varying degrees in all living beings. I was stung by bees last year because I accidentally disturbed their construction of their hive. Kamikaze-like they dove at me in response to danger, by instinct, with intense energy and *élan*, and out of love for their own bee-loud hive. They acted in unison, and with singleminded drive and determination.

Gandhi's political use of Satyagraha as Truth Force, is a lofty human example of Creative Power at work. Indeed Satyagraha as Truth Force in an enlarged capitalized sense can be said to be the mythical power of Love, and of Life itself. Paul Tillich's concept of the power of being leans toward having the same atomic resonance and the same vast embrace of all individual beings. It can also be understood as the power of becoming, and hence as Life itself. It is this Creative Good, the power of being, Truth Force, Life itself, that is the real instance of the abstract Platonic concept of Life.

Let us take five, Pilgrim, for this short postlude at the end of these rather dense philosophical thoughts. Last week I heard a train in the middle of the night carrying oil from the refinery. I hope these very pages will be a train carrying its own freight of meaning to guide you on your own journey. May they help unleash the Creative Power that is manifest in you, and that is indeed coincident with your own creativity. Know that your own creativity is itself Creative Power, a spark from the Divine Fire. Be warned to avoid my own excesses, but be empowered for the uncertain times ahead. Fortunate to be counseled, chastised, and inspired by so many, I am impelled to pass on this small cup of learning to you.

When I heard that train, I had actually been awakened earlier from sleep by the muffled, soothing hooting of an owl, and I was recalling the snow owls that Cuchulain and I heard in the Garden of the Knowledge of Good and Evil. Then it stopped, as if it knew that some behemoth was on its way. Better to let that monster pass, it thought, before I resume my ululations. The rumbling train came with its draconic blasts at each crossing. When the noise died I heard the owl again as if it was very far away. It was really somewhere close by.

21

The Hudson

Archbishop Oscar Romero had just been assassinated

IN THOSE DAYS THERE was actually still another river that brought me sustenance and hope, albeit in an oblique, backhanded way, of which I would not be fully aware till many years later. I am often slow to learn what I do learn, but in this case the river continued to run.

The search committee continued its search for a senior pastor. There was some talk that I was being considered for the position, but I knew that I was not mature enough to be a serious candidate. The search committee obviously did not think so either. Some day you will be ready, said a voice within me, but you are far from ready now.

I was clearly unable to match the cultural and personal expectations of this wealthy group of mainly White women and men who dressed fashionably at home and for church and for their professional jobs in Manhattan, who appeared to have orderly and flourishing family lives, who spoke fluently about fine foods and wines, the country club, the sleeping giant China, investing in the local symphony, and who were most of them American citizens by birth and did not have an accent. None of these things was true of me. The Hudson River stretched between me and them, and neither they nor I could imagine a bridge to yonder shore.

My sermons, still reaching for the moon, still trying to impress, still flowery and theatrical, did not feel grounded. Some were better and braver, advocating concern for the environment and solidarity with the oppressed

The Hudson

in a stodgy punditistic church and culture. Archbishop Oscar Romero had just been assassinated by right-wing death squads in San Salvador, and I was given to profiling him, Henry David Thoreau, Martin Luther King Jr., and Gandhi. The movie *Gandhi* arrived and I took a group to see it in Manhattan. The group sat in grave silence all the way through the long list of credits at the end.

The Hudson River appeared wider than ever when the new senior pastor came on board. I will call him Matthew instead of using his real name. Matthew did seem sure of himself professionally, emotionally, intellectually. I was given to believe that he was a Tillichian in his theology, and his sermons did occupy an abstract conceptual space. What I heard was secularistic sermons that rebuked traditional doctrines of God and Christ by largely snubbing them.

I grant to my pilgrim readers that I was flabbergasted by what I saw and heard. Matt defied all my preconceptions of what a minister should be and do. Disarrayed in my personal life, and carrying no small ego and professional hubris and theological baggage and bias of my own, I could at first admit of no wisdom or inspiration in his sermons. From the start I was jealous, though not quite willing to admit it at the time, and there was nothing more nor less than a stand-off between him and me.

But thoughtful preparations did indeed actually go into Matt's reflections on human nature, false religion, and the good life. I heard comments on how well crafted those sermons were. They did seem honest and original, and evinced intellectual sophistry and a gift for the written word, all of which made an impact on the congregation. They evoked seriousness of intent. There was no drama, flurry, or flair in his sermons or their delivery, nor in his prayers or pulpit manner, nor in the office or in the way he dressed or talked. Only the impatient, perfunctory *tooff- tooff- tooff* half-whistle as he looked for a piece of paper in his desk.

I was chagrined, however, by the change in the order of worship. Matt had no interest in the growing ecumenical liturgical consensus on the place and significance in the historic order of, say, the offerings in relation to the reading of scripture and the spoken word. Nor did he use the lectionary readings. Matt did the pulpit-centered order in which the sermon was the climax. Absent was any emphasis on sacrament. Talk of a sacramental existence was something that was alien to his way of thinking. I personally needed something of a sacramental complement to the spoken word in worship, though I was not always sure myself what that meant in practice.

Matt did his own linear philosophical thinking on these matters in what I considered in isolation, though he was careful not to upset longstanding practice in that local church.

But the people accepted him gladly. The congregation was hungry for sure direction, stability, and emotional strength in their pastor above all things, given their recent experience with the senior pastor. I was shaken by this, and now more than ever I became painfully aware of how I was not able to provide these essentials myself for the church.

I could not make up my mind about Matt at the time, nor did I really try. I detected no telltale signs of trouble in his marriage or louche in his personal life. There was nothing sly about him. He seemed constitutionally exalted above the fray of politics and ideology and even theology. Though he was younger than me and about the same size, he cast a cold, sardonic eye on my life in slow-motion demolition. He seemed to see and know everything, my guilt, my depression, my ignorance, my moral ineptitude. He had something of an angle on me. What was I deflecting by playing prophet? What was I hiding behind my Dr. Zero theological exterior? Behind my cigarette smoke? No wonder he showed no interest in my theological manuscript. For him I was uninteresting and had nothing to say.

His sermons frequently found their mark in my solar plexus. It's not what you know, they said, it's how you live. Those sermons were written for me, sitting in my black academic robe on the other side of the chancel. Do what you must do to order your life properly. If you cannot, your mythical palace of theory is doomed and will soon be revealed as a castle in the sand. The choir and the organist in the choir loft on my left were listening carefully. I wondered what they and the congregation were thinking.

Do you hear my improbable song of a severe and negative light still shining across the years, Pilgrim? And it was not just the verbal message, but the yonder shore of Matt's successful career itself, whose span from my own decrepit cottage was as wide as the Hudson River. After I left the church, excerpts from Matt's sermons were in the church's newsletters. Over the years, they got surer of their substance, always parsing away the fine points of their author's own thinking. There was courage in this. Matt was true to himself in his sermons. There seemed no end to what I could learn from this man, though I could never admit this back then.

I myself used fragments from his sermons at times. The story of Boethius was compelling. Wrongfully imprisoned and executed by the Ostrogoth Theodoric, Arian king of Italy, he produced his masterpiece *On the Consolation of Philosophy* while languishing in prison. Unjust suffering may yet not destroy one's tranquility when one allows the bright forms Fortitude and Goodness to gladden one's days. Boethius also followed in the footsteps of Plato.

When I delivered my own sermon on Boethius, the congregation sat riveted. Something about it must have resonated with them as it did with me. I was saying that we are all Boethius. We know what it is to languish in prison and to think our own thoughts on the meaning of these days. It is our way of fighting back against the Ostrogoth.

I beckon the Platonic forms through my writing and reading and teaching and listening to music, and the Ostrogoth king withdraws, green with envy. He knows I participate through these activities in Truth and Beauty, which brighten my days in the gloom of my prison. The Ostrogoth king fumes when I lift up my heart in worship. I am never closer to Integrity and Wholeness and Transcendence than when I am with the worshiping community, and these set my soul on fire. And when I do acts of Justice and Kindness and, in Solidarity with my fellow creatures, serve a cup of cold water, lead an advocacy task force, or preach on the blighted lives of the poor or on the protection of our wild lands and wild waters and wild creatures, the Ostrogoth knows that Justice and Kindness are immanent in my heart, and that in my heart the sun is shining when it is cold and bleak outside, and hope is raging when there is no reason to hope.

Matt's sermons continued to resist pronouncements or be shaken by the pull and push and pressure of the cosmos. They remained brainy, dry, detached, and serene, as if to send a certain sharp and austere message, which was working well with the congregation as far as I knew. Photographs of Matt with confirmation youth and families joining the church appeared regularly in the newsletters. He never relinquished his power. The church prospered.

22

Puget Sound

Comfort the sorrowing and stand in solidarity with the weak and the powerless

A DIVORCE TOOK PLACE in Seattle. It was inevitable. Long gone was the day when the passion of love was paramount and nothing else mattered. What made the dissolution of our marriage possible was that the church would not be an obstructive factor. This was in the middle of the big postmodern city, it was early in my ministry there, and she herself initiated the action. Nobody seemed to notice, as if everyone knew the story anyway. The days of wine and roses passed away, and for a while the ecstasy of freedom and the abyss of despondency both held sway. Someone had released me and someone had been wrenched away. A door banged shut somewhere in the Gothic house. A door marked Nevermore.

I cannot deny my shakenness and weakness, as if I had just awoken in a recovery room after a traumatic surgery. The contradictory emotions with which I had long awaited this moment roiled the waters of my soul. When the moment actually came I was not prepared. Reason would have halted the relationship from the beginning, but the River of No Return had plunged uncontrollably over the edge. The stillness now of the house was not the stillness of sweet solitude, nor the silence the sacred silence of the monastery in Snowmass, where the monks speak not a word except in chants and liturgy. No, it was not long before the dark night creatures of the sky, invisible to the naked eye, delivered Self-pity and Concupiscence to the door of the big parsonage. I was left again to brood upon the void and the darkness that covered the waters.

I fled to the University arboretum and its abundant preserve of shrubs and trees and network of nature trails and murmuring brooks for comfort and crying. Would that I could drown myself in the dark face of those Lake Washington inlets, and then rise from the waters a new creation, with the complexion of all the flying, fleeing, leaping, climbing, swimming, growing things of summer. Surely I must know now the secret of sorrow and existence.

I did get to keep the pebbles I had gathered from a beach in Maine. It would be my intention to return them to the same beach, to the seaweed and the sound and spray of the crashing waves. They still sit to this day, however, on my dining and coffee tables. When I look at them I see the ladder that goes down to the beach, and I look out upon the blue sea and hear the loud roar of the sea against the cliffs. I see the cormorants fly north and south and feel the sting of the cold ocean breeze. There are things I had rather not remember too, which I will not recall here.

Yesterday I put my hand upon the pebbles and moved them slightly to convey my thoughts for them of my love. We've been through so much together from the very beginning. They are smooth like marbles to the touch. They are round. One looks like a Volkswagen bug and it still shows dimly the crayon wheels that I once marked on it. I know I cannot possess you, I tell them. I will lay you down gently one day by the waters.

Now it was the Pacific Ocean, the lakes and islands and mountain forests, and a small church here that had called me to Puget Sound. In those days there was a surge of interest in protecting the environment and wildlife habitat. It was the right time and fertile soil for the E. Stanley Jones Himalayan ashram seed within me to grow and bear fruit. Soon I was persuading the Hindu community, the Progressive Animal Welfare Society, Greenpeace, the Church Council of Greater Seattle, and my own church, to have a weekly meeting around the principle of respect for life, both human and nonhuman. In our statement of mission I urged, rather rhetorically, that it was important to do this in an era in which the exploitation of nature is rampant, violence and injustice have become institutionalized, and the human spirit itself has become orphaned in an artificial and technological society.

In fact we did gather weekly for a vegetarian meal and then sit in a circle on the floor in the Learning Community for dialogue, readings from

The Meaning of These Days

the Hindu and Christian texts, chants and silence, leaving our shoes at the door. The Ecology and Theology Task Force, organized under the umbrella of the Church Council of Greater Seattle, arranged conferences, ecumenical services, and Earth Day activities. People from all walks of life came to help us with the Task Force, and the meetings were often crowded.

We arranged for my Claremont professor John Cobb, Jr. to address one of our conferences, and a University of Washington scientist dialogued with us in another. I had come to know and respect Cobb on a personal level, and he was in fact still patiently helping me with my manuscript during my time in Seattle. He had already introduced me to Pilgrim Place, the retirement community of religious professionals in which he resides with his wife Jean in Claremont. I was impressed by the humility with which he commented on my material. In a long and supportive letter he said briefly at the end that he did not always follow my thinking, but that this was a matter of uncertainty rather than disagreement. He offered that the spiritual life seemed more sharply separated from the secular life for me than for him.

At the ashram meetings I read from the introductory pages of *The Liberation of Life* by Birch and Cobb, from Rabindranath Tagore's *Gitanjali*, from Albert Schweitzer's autobiography, and from Sarvapalli Radhakrishnan's writings, masterful revisions and reaffirmations of Eastern thought for both Eastern and Western readers. The Indians in the ashram looked at each other and nodded, speechless. Are we really hearing these words or is this an illusion? We are in the presence of a towering personage, I explained for those who did not know, a famous Oxford lecturer and author, a highly respected ambassador and legislator and statesperson, Indian representative to the United Nations, and President of India.

I read out short, inspiring fragments about how contentment is more desirable than riches, a mind at peace with itself than the applause of assemblies, how the thoughts and lives of the saints and sages of both East and West can speak powerfully to this brave new emancipated world, how our contemporary quandary has resulted from the steady erosion of our moral and spiritual values, and how in the end it falls upon us to comfort the sorrowing and stand in solidarity with the weak and the powerless. The prose soared above religious and ideological boundaries to embrace what an English journalist referred to as the ample air of the Universal Spirit upon hearing one of Radhakrishnan's sermons in an Anglican church.

Puget Sound

The sonorousness and glow of those interfaith vespers was not lost on me. I was the proud but pale preacher instrument through whom those capacious words went out into the night from that small church. As the ferry was approaching the skyline of the twenty-first century, getting bigger and bigger were the oil spills, the overfishing and the clear-cutting of forests worldwide, the ethnic wars with their mass cross-border migrations and refugee camps, the neon and noise of the throw-away I-It economies, and the power of the transnational corporations and the World Trade Organization.

In the end the aims of our several groups, each with its own agenda, proved to be so incongruous with one another that we had no choice but to dissolve the ashram. Upon hearing our emphasis upon respect for life, for example, a person from Greenpeace had asked, Do not rocks deserve respect too? It was a far better question than I was wise enough to admit at the time. The ashram did give birth through the church to a Blessing of the Animals service on St. Francis Day early in October. I felt in my heart that this ashram experiment was one of the best things I had ever done. The spirituality and theology that were still in formation for me would doubtless be affected by it.

Furthermore, I am fairly convinced that my ashram ministry hastened my wife's decision to leave. We had grown increasingly out of favor with one another, and my channeling of my energies elsewhere was a bold statement of my own intentions to make a change in a relationship that had long ceased to be viable. Seattle's economy was resilient, its marketplace was exuberant and progressive, and opportunities abounded, all of which also contributed no doubt to my wife's decision.

The scores of people I met through the ashram were, most of them, high-minded, talented, intelligent persons who cared about the earth and its creatures. One attractive young woman from the Progressive Animal Welfare Society was known to hold the animals in her arms after they had been euthanized. Contrast this, Pilgrim, with the insane cruelty of factory farms tucked far away in the country. Think also of the bodies of beautiful flying, creeping, crawling, burrowing, wading, running beings strewn along our highways. How we speed on by with nary a thought, inured to the victims sometimes having dragged themselves to the margins.

Today hawks and eagles sit on trees and fence posts along the highway waiting for road-kills. They have nowhere else to hunt. The fields, as far as the eye can see, have been plowed. The spread wings of these beautiful birds, now forever still, are also visible at times by the side of the road.

Radhakrishnan was a shy and sensitive person who kept to himself even while passing as quite sociable. His photos reveal a small man with a gentle face and a generous disposition. He got his education in Christian missionary institutions, and it was there that his hurts and doubts, the clash in the chapel between his Hindu identity and the narrow early-twentieth-century message of Christian missionaries, and the tension generally between East and West ignited his philosophy career. In his moving autobiographical sketch *My Search for Truth*, to which I ardently refer my pilgrim readers as must reading, he says that he was annoyed with the derision with which the doctrines of Hindu villagers were treated, and he was offended by the talk of a chosen people and of salvation by no other name.

It was to the credit, however, of Professor A. G. Hogg, the principal of Madras Christian College, that he noted the quality of Radhakrishnan's work and awarded him a testimonial encouraging him in his philosophico-theological studies, in particular his explorations in the *Vedanta*. Radhakrishnan was twenty at the time, and he was always to prize that tribute dearly.

Reading Radhakrishnan on Hogg brings tears of ecstasy and joy and even pride to my eyes. Of all the Christian missionaries I have known or heard of, he was among the noblest, wisest, and most just, to use the words that Plato used for Socrates. What a witness to Christ and to the Christian faith that he should commend to a young man the study of the texts of his own religion. He was in a position to commend, instead, the study of the Christian texts or of Christian theologians. He could have tried to persuade Radhakrishnan of the superiority of the Christian narrative over the highest speculations of Eastern thought, and to offer conversion and be sent to Oxford or Cambridge as a reward. But no, he was an empathetic, educated, and enlightened man, and he knew better than to offer bribes and make false claims.

Radhakrishnan was aware that in his writings he was withholding the sorrows, secrets, and anxieties of his personal life from us, and he justified his reticence by invoking Robert Browning's distinction between the self you present to the public and the self you reveal to the one you love. This distinction is an interesting variant of several related oppositions with which we are now familiar, I and Thou versus I and It, the gulf between intellect and existence, between the seminary and the city, and between word and flesh, the chasm between the logosphere and the River of No Return, between yonder shore and hither shore, form and feeling, and male and female, the juxtaposition of the person of heaven and the person of dust, and the divide between the lion loose and the lion captured.

We might want to add to the above contradictions T.S. Eliot's division between the person who suffers and the mind which creates. The sexual tension between the two poles or foci of these several divides in the ellipse is just the mystery of the Creative Good, though polarization can affect the process adversely, dragging both sides down, as we have seen.

Aside from avowing his indignation at the Christian missionaries of his early years, Radhakrishnan's world climbs steeply to the Himalayan bliss of the logosphere, Plato's heaven of forms. The pursuing army of the dreaded black-robed demons Angst and Warp and Decadence are left behind in the desert valley to grovel among the dry bones of their own dead. Sorrows and secrets are silent, but the serenity of love and understanding and good will is the fine Brahmanic dust that has settled on everything. It is the air you breathe at Radhakrishnan's mountain retreat. The Truth is not in the earthquake, wind, and fire. It is when you put your ear to the ground that you hear a heartbeat, barely audible, far, far away.

23

Middle Path

*Moth and rust corrupted and thieves
broke through to steal*

AGAIN I WENT INTO therapy, this time with a difference. I knew it would be for the long haul. I had stopped smoking when the patch first came on the market. That victory gave me the animus I needed to seek order in my life. I knew that the relationship between my private life and my public life was still a rabble of irresolution and discontent. Suppression had become the womb of desire, and the connection between the two was the broth in which the demons cooked this pastor's meal of shame and remorse at the close of day. The embattled spark of Truth within me was helpless to contain the lusts which tainted the sermons and degraded the pastoral care and leadership I was able to provide. The war raged in Kurukshetra between word and flesh. Moth and rust corroded and thieves broke through to steal not just the treasures of earth but also the treasures of heaven.

Luke is the name I will give my pastoral counselor. From my internship in Atlanta with the Georgia Association of Pastoral Care I had come to trust the training pastoral counselors receive, and Luke did turn out to be intelligent, professional, and compassionate. Even though he was considerably younger than me, his style was to listen to my problems and then try patiently, step by step, to teach me elementary truths about self-destructive patterns versus a sagacious and healthy life. Not necessarily a normal life, he would point out, but a healthy life. There was also the important distinction between immediate needs and long-term goals. The money spent on

Middle Path

his house, being an investment, he explained, served a long-term goal. Luke also emphasized that actions have consequences, that it is impossible to undo an action, and that there are more similarities than there are differences between women and men. These were such simple and basic principles. The task now would be to grow them inwardly and let them bear fruit. Let them become living water within me bubbling up into abundant life.

I did find the last point about women and men difficult, though we did not talk much about it. Was Luke himself entirely convinced of its truth? Do not men sometimes see in a woman threatening beauty? Sometimes feel trembling desire? Sometimes hear the sea's roar of love? But I submitted willingly to his tutorials because I knew I needed them. He did not hesitate to tell me No when I asked him about the tall and attractive Kristen who worked at the Honey Bear Bakery. After weeks of my glances in her direction, she had introduced herself to me, and there seemed to me a mutual attraction between us. I brought this matter to Luke, wondering whether I should pursue her. You are too old for her, Luke said bluntly and with an air of finality. Again, I gave him the benefit of the doubt, which kept nagging at me and dragging me to the bakery for scones and coffee. I still think of Kristen, but I know that Luke was right.

If it did not completely transform me, just the fact that I was seeing Luke on a regular basis provided me a measure of stability and self-esteem. When my father came to visit me, I took him with me to see Luke, who by now knew my story well. I asked my father to tell Luke what he had told me about my mother and him in New Delhi. He hesitated for a long time and then confessed haltingly that it was too painful to repeat. That one time near the Gol Market bazaar was not to be replicated.

My father's eyesight was failing. At the airport terminal there had been a crowd, and he came into the clearing and the glare of the lights waiting to hear my voice. Dad! I said loudly, Dad! We hugged and he commented on how my London Fog overcoat was fetching. He was getting old now. I regret having him stay upstairs. He should have had the main floor, which had a full bath and a full-size bed. Remembering him climb up the dark narrow stairs holding onto the railing saddens me deeply.

This would be the last time that my father would visit here. I did go and see him in Ludhiana a few years later. He was not well. He would lie and listen to the BBC broadcasts over the radio and pace up and down between the old school and the parsonage. I accompanied him to the Christian Medical College hospital across the busy honking street from the leafy mission compound. He told me that the doctors were not quite sure what was causing the infection and the rise in temperature.

That mission compound, lush with its flowering vines and red-leaf plants, was the scene of my earliest memories. I learned the poetic Urdu script on a slate in that school in kindergarten to the sound of mynahs, parrots, nightingales, woodpeckers, and chicadees in the yard and in the shade of the big palm and neem and pipal and other tropical trees. We could see the big bungalow which housed the American missionaries and their beautiful children with their many-colored T-shirts and red and blue and yellow bicycles with fat tires and back-pedal brakes. We were never invited into the bungalow but, at least later in Ferozepore in a similar setting, the children came to us.

The residences of doctors and nurses and other hospital staff and missionary personnel were also in the compound, as was the church at which my father was pastor back then too. On Sundays there was always an English service in the evening and a crowded Hindustani service in the morning. It was in the church and the parsonage yards that I first knew the daily fragrance of marigolds, petunias, pansies, roses, and sweet peas. The gardener always kept one eye on me. The scent of jasmine drifted upon the breeze in the evening, as did the lilting Lata Mangeshkar songs of love and loneliness.

It was past sunset and dark when the *tonga* arrived to take me to the railway station. I always hated saying goodbye though I had said it a thousand times by now to my family on platforms and had watched them grow smaller and smaller as the train pulled away. This time there was just my dad and me alone. The old servant Phillip, my beloved Aunt Ta, who had been living with my mom and dad in her old age, and my mom herself had all died. It was fortunate that my dad still had the church to care about him. Again I hated this moment and held my grief and my sudden trembling at bay as usual as I hugged him and said goodbye in the darkness. There was a marked slowness and quietness about him this time. It was not a slowness and quietness unto death, I think, but unto a final and unutterable sadness. He knew that this was the last goodbye. I walked with my backpack out through the compound gate, where the tonga waited. It was, I suspect, too much for me to bear for both of us.

Back in America Luke and I talked about politics as well as my personal life, and we disagreed about the first war in Iraq and the elder George Bush. I agreed with him on Reaganomics and American militarism but did

Middle Path

not think that Bush was a sociopath like Saddam Hussein. At that time I was hearing among other things about the torture and rape of the Kuwaitis after Saddam's invasion of their country. I also found myself in a maelstrom of politics in the church and community. I had to explain that I did espouse the Gandhian principle of nonviolence even though I was not a pacifist in the full philosophical sense, which admits of no exceptions whatever. The peace activists by whom I was surrounded, however, were in no mood for such a fine distinction, and could not bear or even hear it. I saw a shadow darken one woman's face and glaze her eyes on the thought of her son going to war. She was not one to scream, but I thought I heard the echoes of one in her soul.

I meet today in this town where I live with a peace group consisting of retired Church of the Brethren pacifist pastors and others. The moral perversity of regarding the trauma of war lightly is what joins me to this group. With them too I have made the same distinction as above, but they do not seem to care, nor do they really understand.

In the late twentieth century the world was adrift. Things were adding up, the consequences of a harsh free market ideology were coming in, and families were facing increasing social stress and financial hardship. In troubled times how easy it is to go to extremes for comfort and peace of mind. When tsunamic waves beat relentlessly on the shore we take shelter in some absolute that promises relief from the agitations of mind and heart.

In Seattle I met many such refugees who had found their ultimate saint or church or philosophy. There was the softspoken, gentle, and brilliant Hindu man under psychiatric care, who attended our ashram and worshiped through his own guru privately at home. He borrowed my copy of Zaehner's commentary on the *Bhagavad Gita* at my suggestion, but returned it politely, without comment. On the winding blue highway through the North Cascades National Park he could not understand the idea of many different centers and sources of truth and nurture, or of a community of faith making important spiritual decisions in dialogue.

Another man, who was part of our informal men's group that met spontaneously at the Honey Bear Bakery, saw the world exclusively through the eyes of Noam Chomsky and resorted finally to bringing me some of Chomsky's photocopied pages. A third person disrupted our ashram meeting rudely and lectured to us of the scandal of such worship in a Christian church. Still another laughed and dismissed other churches than his own as at best derivative and inferior forms of Christian faith and practice.

The Meaning of These Days

Meanwhile, driven by my own rage for order, my theological manuscript had likewise gotten bogged down in a foggy marsh of misdirection. I knew it was trying to drift toward some mother lode of mystical truth in which all contradictions would be finally resolved and all rivers become one in the ocean of being, and it was John Cobb's reservations about my third and final stage of the spiritual life that confirmed my own doubts.

I had also begun to doubt the first two stages as stages. The one thing I was clear about was the conflict between the lion-loose and the lion-captured theological alternatives, and that there was truth both in the former existentialistic neo-orthodox type option and the latter liberal philosophical type option. That there was falsehood in both camps also was amply and importantly confirmed for me by the ugly and destructive extremists I had met from both. I felt strongly about the need for a middle path, which would take the place of the ousted third stage. The fog had thickened, however, when I got to writing down what such a path might look like.

Paul Tillich had reached this same impasse in his small book about Biblical religion and the philosophical search for ultimate reality. Tillich's greatness was his ability to give each alternative a persuasive hearing, but the most he could do was to point those of us who could accept neither extreme exclusively toward carrying on the theological project on the border between abyss and ground.

On my mind was also Niebuhr's existentialistic dialectic between the children of light and the children of darkness, between spirit and nature, between rational ideals and the manifest scenarios of power and politics. They too were germane for any adequate reading of the spiritual quandary. This kind of oppositional meta-language of Niebuhr and Tillich seemed more and more to me to ring true to the *sturm und drang* of human experience. I therefore consigned myself to the modest task of navigating the dangers on the streets of Laredo, while yet keeping an eye out for striking a rapturous, if ephemeral, chord of harmony between the two cultures.

24

Mount Rainier

A voice said, Cry! And I said, What shall I cry?

THE EARLY YEARS OF the twenty-first century have been described by Jane Kramer in *The New Yorker* as fierce theological times, with fundamentalism's claimed sole purchase on truth, its contempt for the moral accommodation of liberal Western secularism, its strong imperative to censure and convert, and its alleged monopoly of heaven. She does not mention the individualism and privatism that are often associated with such extremism.

Kramer is writing about Islamic fundamentalism, but extremist ideologies on the right in the United States in the late twentieth century were also resurgent. As pastor I could feel the violence of social stress and financial hardship on American families, and homelessness was on the rise. The unconscionable decision during the recession of the seventies to cut services for the mentally ill was now taking its toll, and the country's political stamina to deal with this *reductio ad absurdum* of the unbridled growth economy was nonexistent.

We would also hear about bears disoriented by the clear-cutting and the housing developments in woods that were pristine and primal, the home of abundant wildlife. The burgeoning environmental movement was facing its own teenage traumas as it faced down the loggers of the timber industry. I traveled everywhere in the mountains and valleys and to the islands and the seashore dreaming of land out of easy reach that I myself could afford. In the end I trembled as I parted with my meager savings for one acre in the Christmas tree wilderness. It would be my escape from the city's arrows that fly by day and the pestilence that stalks by night.

The Meaning of These Days

But back home a voice cried out in the urban desert. The homeless man who became my next teacher, and whom I will call Paul, was tall and muscular and virulent. He was a walker and was known by the city and the churches. He knew the location of the garbage cans and the shelters, and he knew the dangers and the secrets of the streets.

When he was in our church on Sunday mornings he sat outside the sanctuary in the lobby entrance. The wild currents surrounding Alcatraz were the currents that separated Paul from the world. Was it his raspy voice? His inability to engage rationally or emotionally? His attire, his beard, his personal hygiene? I tried letting him use my refrigerator and sleep in the basement of the parsonage on the condition that he did not bring in cans or used paper or styrofoam cups or plates, plastic bottles, or cardboard scraps, let alone discarded furniture. It did not work. I found a closet filled to the brim with all these things and a broken living room chair. Water for tea was left boiling on the burner but forgotten about.

But no one saw as piercingly as Paul the mindless wastefulness of our throw-away society. Were they possessive or creative, his acts of picking up scraps on the streets? Were they sin and creation in the same act? The layers of heedlessness were as omnipresent to Paul as racism is to a person who is black or brown.

Let us let Paul sit where he wants to sit. It is in this church and some others he experiences remnants of I and Thou, hints of the inexhaustible ground of being, and a certain will to do justly and fill the hungry with good things. He hears *Sheep May Safely Graze* and the singing of *Savior, Like a Shepherd Lead Us* through the door and indeed he feels secure in these churches. Or is it a church person who breathed a warm word earlier in the parking lot or in the building itself? The street brutishness on Paul's face is replaced now by the Sabbath rest by Galilee and the silence of eternity. On the streets Paul's bearing is sullen and bestial. Here it is almost childlike in its innocence and softness, and broodingly anticipatory and receptive. Is there any violence here? He does not feel it. Is there any abandonment, any banishment into the cold, cold night, any disgust or condemnation as there was once, perhaps, when he was young? He does not know it. Let him sit and be at peace.

A voice said, Cry, and I said, What shall I cry?

Though I was encouraged by the work of my friends on the motley issues of justice and the environment, the problem of freedom of thought kept flaring up for me in the sky like Mount Rainier on a clear day. Angry pressures upon us to conform cause us to become negative, to detach ourselves like Thoreau and march to the beat of a different drummer, step to the music of our own conscience, and find a way to transcend the threat to our integrity and our very selfhood by some yogic or philosophic or religious engagement with logos, while at the same time the erotic loneliness for the world persists. In transcending, said Thoreau, we will pass an invisible boundary and find ourselves in the company of a higher order of beings.

I felt the radioactivity of detachment and *eros* deeply in Seattle, which made me even clearer and surer of Tillich's and Niebuhr's point and counterpoint, thesis and antithesis way of rendering such internal dissonance. We can reread this existential jaggedness in a softer, rounder, feminist way perhaps by understanding it as a cycle or upward spiral connecting opposing foci over the long term, or even as a migration on the broad biodiverse canvas of life between word and world. Theological discourse may thus accommodate the non-masculine epiphanies of literature, art, and music.

In describing his third way, Tillich advocated probing toward a synthesis of the *via negativa* and the *via moderna*. But did he not know? Had he not heard how fugitive and sometimes phantom are the blissful unions of freedom and bonding, detachment and love, male and female? Lovers see how quickly their frolic ends. Pilgrims cannot possess their mountaintop or seashore ecstasies. Politicians discover how impossible are the infinite demands of justice and how fluid their compromises. Artists speak of the horizon perennially receding, and modern composers know that enchantment, innocence, and wholeness are now behind them. In the words of the music critic Alex Ross about Shostakovich and the twentieth century, the honest soul wavers now between solitary brooding and heedless release. Even so, it may be said that this foreplay upon the waters occurs just so that the pleasure note of enchantment and the resonant chord of wholeness can be struck again and again in new ways.

The middle path between solitude and desire is thus a shifting balance, forever correcting itself with arms waving as on a beam in the gymnasium. Some of us consult with counselors and doctors to learn to walk the beam skillfully. There is a back and forth between essence and existence. The professional's world is an I and It world of therapies and scientific terms, but when we actually apply the cream of what we learn to the flesh of our lives there is an occurrence of I and Thou, a union of abstraction and the stream of life, a fluid and pragmatic seamlessness between transcendent form and immanent function.

We also know just how temporary such fixes can be, and that we are in the gymnasium for the long haul. A secure place in the sun with no disequilibrium, no cause to be repelled into transcendence, and no erotic pull downward into immanence, blocks the wild wind of creation. No fear of the terror of the night or the arrow that flies by day, and no tumult of love or travail of loss, becomes an arrested and disenchanted existence.

25

The Whirlwind

'Tis seven long years since last I've seen you

I HAVE LONG FUSED the telling of my journey with my musings about religion, God, and the vexed meaning of these days. Could it be that my natural inclination to muse has been an underlying reason why I studied philosophy, became a pastor, and started the manuscript which has finally morphed into this extended meditation? In this chapter I will ramble a bit and reflect further on the lessons I have learned and about the questions that continue to surface for me and hold my attention.

All through the book I have written, in particular, about the generic dualisms that have both assailed my journey and spurred it forward. These right hand and left hand, breathing in and breathing out, negative and positive cross-currents stir up the perfect storm for new creation. The mention of new creation leads, of course, to the idea of God as Creative Process, Creative Good, Life itself, Satyagraha, and for this basic idea I am grateful to the process tradition in theology.

To include Satyagraha in the list is my own choice. Satyagraha harbors at least a potential opposition in its very name, as *satya* means Truth and *graha* Power. It is not enough to know the Truth. Truth must be lived out often against the turbulence of real time. Creative Good evokes a child building something with logo pieces amid the actual clutter of created goods all around her. The Creative Wind moves upon troubled waters in the darkness before the first light dawns and a green order emerges.

We are contemplating Life itself as a mystery that scientists and writers, theologians and philosophers, pilgrims and worshipers all seek to understand. Is this mystery truly God Godself, as we have suggested in a preceding chapter? Is this the uncontrollable mystery on the bestial floor that the magi in Yeats' poem seek, being by Calvary's turbulence unsatisfied? After preaching sermons every Sunday for so many years and looking every week at other options from all sides, for me all signs point to the overwhelmingly affirmative answer: What better way to apprehend the ultimate mystery than as the mystery of Life itself, the Creative Good? What can be worthier of our personal devotion and of corporate worship? Is not this, then, the answer to the question of the Eternal and Universal Thou?

Some say that the study of Life is a purely scientific discipline. Yet despite the heroic claims of the scientistic despisers of religion that questions about Life have been domesticated, that the matter of origins has been tamed biochemically in the laboratory, and that even the hemoglobin of long-extinct animals has now been synthesized, the subject of Life has hardly come closer to being exhausted. It cries out for a contemplative response, which may take a literary, mythic, musical, poetic, philosophical, or religious form.

It is when the work is done in the laboratory and Dr. DNA steps out into the dark stillness of the night that the large questions of Life haunt him again and again, questions about simple human gestures that he ponders, and about other daily, ordinary things about which he has only suspicions, and which always seem to have hidden meanings or motives. This fragrant wisp of north wind, whence does it come and whither does it go? Why do my emotions have an intensity incommensurate with the outward reality that corresponds with them, and why does my conduct sometimes have a mind of its own? How have my wife, my children, my brother, and others come to have such power over me?

As he walks in the starry, starry night he also broods about the moral and philosophical questions about science and technology themselves, and about the interconnectedness of all things. How deep does our knowledge really go? He has been given to worrying about the estimated 210,000 gallons of oil that gushed every day mercilessly and uncontained into the Gulf of Mexico. He remembers the fiery conflagration on the vessel that sent eleven people to their deaths and injured seventeen others, and how the flames and the soot leapt up to the heights of the sky. Now what remains is the clumps of reddish tar and a black blob. Was this just another warning that we must change our ways? Is not the real problem much deeper than the deepest sea?

The Whirlwind

Dr. DNA is known affectionately as The Double Helix by the staff and faculty in the huge university research laboratory. He walks home to his own leafy neighborhood miles away feeling quite alone in the world. He has been working late for years on Tuesdays and Thursdays and does not notice the occasional car that goes by on this stretch of his walk any longer. Lately a strange sense of gloom has come to occupy his mind. He stops, as he usually does, at the creek which borders the area of his home and where the road makes a turn. The big cottonwoods and cedars here, two types of trees that he loves, form a dome, a symphony hall, and the running water and the hushed breeze are music to his ears.

He remembers how Henri Bergson said that in order to understand something you have to intuit yourself inside it. So he stands on the narrow wooden bridge that crosses the mellifluous stream and takes in the sound. How ravenous and unconfinable our mental capacities, yet how impossible to describe the meaning and beauty of what he hears. Silent and tender is the descent of a falling leaf, he thinks, and gentle and light its journey upon the water, and we are helpless to render it in words. How little we really know in such a fluid world of process and change. Are we not specks of dust against the twinkling heavens, and yet how much damage we do.

As he stands on the bridge his thoughts begin to wander again as to whether the experts have really fixed the broken well in the deep and dark unknown approximately one mile down to the bottom of the sea, and how extensive the damage will ultimately be to the fragile ecosystems, the wildlife preserves, the spawning grounds, the marshes and swamps and bayous and beaches along the coastline. Many species of birds, including the endangered brown pelicans and different types of terns, migrate and nest here. And what about the fish and turtles and alligators and other wetland animals? But this melancholy, he realizes, is just the tip of the iceberg of his doldrums. There is something deeper, an angst that he has long given up trying to comprehend or control.

Thus does Dr. DNA exercise his own contemplations about Life outside the laboratory. Anticipating and even encouraging a congregation to engage not just in a personalistic way of doing religion but also in a contemplative response to the uncontrollable mystery, my own prayers in church today often address God in one breath suggestively as the Mother and Father of all beings and as the Creative Power of the cosmos. All my sermons are grounded in the open assumption that God is the depth of the Creative Process itself, and that God's Spirit is the underlying current of

Life within us. It makes a huge difference when we regard our own thoughts and feelings, our own joys and anxieties and sorrows, as thus also part of the Divine Life itself. Our suffering is also God's suffering. Our bliss is also God's bliss.

It is through us as living beings that God does God's creative work. This Easter I preached on the appearance of the Mysterious Stranger on the beach before the break of dawn. Cast your net on the other side, he says loudly, knowing that the toiling disciples have not caught any fish. In my sermon I emphasized that we must understand the risen Christ not in the linear, literalistic language of dogmatic religion, nor in the ecstatic, rapturous language of shallow religion, but give me a Christ, I said, who reminds us to love our enemies, to bless those who persecute us, and in this way to move the process of reconciliation forward. They who hunger and thirst after righteousness, justice, and peace are truly blessed because it is they who advance the world creatively toward the abundance of life. Easter is the glorious affirmation that Death shall have no dominion over the creativity of Jesus.

These and other prayers and sermons and stories I prepare are not only in keeping with the aim of the creation stories of Genesis One and Two, but it is my hope that they broaden and liberate the religious framework of the people of the church, whatever their background might be, and that they help ground the religiousness of the people in deep I and Thou Relatedness, in the disciplined practice of Goodness, and in a rich, earthy kind of body-and-mind Wholeness of the Gospel narratives.

Unabashedly I tell the world what the Welsh poet Dylan Thomas knew, that the force that through the green fuse drives the flower, that drives our red blood and our green age, is the same Force that powers us to sing in our chains like the sea, the same Force that shatters the stranglehold of the past, buckles the power of the night, and lures us to rise at dawn, go for the walk in the stadium against the morning rain and wind, and clutch to our bosom the forgiveness of a new day.

Is God personal? It is a delicate question. To be personal is more than just being an individual. It is to be caught up in the power of being and becoming. In the eighth century CE the Indian philosopher Sankara developed his nondualistic metaphysics of Brahman as nonpersonal undifferentiated being. The philosopher Ramanuja in the eleventh century CE, however, insisted that Brahman is personal. Ramanuja was more nearly right only in the limited sense that that the manifestations of Life are

The Whirlwind

indeed personal beings, both human and nonhuman. As personal beings, however, they are taken up into the Living Process, which is their essence. Human beings evince Satyagraha by unleashing the power of Truth against the grain of empire. It is who and what they are. In the larger and general sense, are not all beings, both personal and nonpersonal, expressions of the mystery of Satyagraha, the Creative Process? And has not Martin Buber taught us that any entity whatever can be addressed as a personal Thou?

It can do no harm but only good to extrapolate that the pebbles and the sand and even the washed up bottles and paper cups on the beaches of rivers and oceans are entities deserving interest or respect. Do they not contain messages from an invisible yonder shore? And if we so consider them, will we not treat them with a certain regard and tenderness, each as a Thou, instead of an object to be thrown away, used and discarded? We treasure even the tools we use and protect them from thieves and rust. Do not created goods carry the hope that the Goodness which produced them will endure in and through them, and that they too will interact with other goods and participate in the compost of Life itself? Cannot the cup be used again and again in the soft-rock ambience of Starbucks, and is not the food we prepare and eat absorbed by a Process vastly greater than the food itself?

I have toiled, and will always toil, to bring pellucidity to my own life. It was in Seattle that I resolved for moral and spiritual reasons to submit myself to counseling for the long term. For one thing, it would give me someone to be accountable to. I have kept my promise. At the time of this writing I am far from Seattle. Here I have found a spiritual director in the big city close by to be my counselor. I will call her Mary. I hear from her about constructive steps I can take to cope with the torments and troubles that still plague me and thus to move my own life creatively forward. Decorate the house with a new table cloth. Buy a CD player and CDs and listen to music. Listening to music, I remember, was something that the pastoral counselor Luke in Seattle had also urged. Visit the wildlife preserve near the town where you live, says Mary, and feast your eyes on the land in all directions from the tower. Approach your church work, your reading and writing, your bicycling and walking to the college and the church, your cooking and even housecleaning, as forms of yoga, spiritual discipline, prayer.

I trust Mary's female energy as well as her intelligence. She is widely read in contemplative and feminist studies. The actions she urges are in origin an open revolt against the unbearability of sin, though the table cloth and the music and the prairie and wildlife preserve can be a pleasure in and of themselves. While she suggests them as a *via negativa*, a firewall against the tree of burning desire, they are also a *via moderna*, a positive embrace of color and sound and landscape.

My counselor's idea is to forge a path less forbidding than a permanent medieval dark night of the soul, a via negativa opposed always to delight and desire. So in the darkness and solitude of this humble house I brood on some of the mature songs of Bob Dylan, the ungrounded and irreverent melodious musicality of John Lennon's son Sean, Chanticleer's rendition of *Shenandoah* and *We Shall Walk Through the Valley in Peace*, Gabriella Montero's piano improvisations of Bach, Gregorian chants. *Shenandoah* takes me back to Montgomery Hall in San Anselmo, where I heard it down the hallway for the first time. *'Tis seven long years since last I've seen you*, cry the singers to the rolling river and the smiling valley. I hear the words sung and my own eyes dissolve in tears. A refuge from our own striving, music is a welcome blend of meaning and matter, detachment and delight, ideal and real.

We are now back on the subject of middle ground. The spiritual task is to forge just the middle path the counselor urges between the via negativa and the via moderna, between the flight from boredom, anxiety, and addiction on the one hand, and on the other, the rapture of the Sabbath ringing slowly in the holy streams, the joys of love and landscape, of literature, the arts, and music, and of learning about the remaining wilderness areas and the wolves and lions in the mountains. Scary, steep, and foggy was Damnation Creek that came down the North Cascades in the west, but in the east was the smiling valley and rolling river. An old many-sided cabin was there, built by the hippies in the sixties. It nestled on a grassy bench in the Ponderosa mountains near a small trickling creek, and it had bats and bees and butterflies.

The leapfrogging, migrating, spiralling, sometimes blending patterns of revulsion and desire, flight and return, seclusion and submergence, are the anarchic reason and artistic essence of the Whirlwind God. The very objects of desire come tagged with warnings that make a leopard pause in its leap. The seminary of San Anselmo and the city of San Francisco become metaphysical entities separated by the raging waters and mutually accessible on the Golden Gate Bridge of Transcendence.

The clients and the young waiters and waitresses look to see who is playing *In the Still of the Night* in the cineplex diner juke box. I am reminded of the Greyhound bus terminal in San Francisco. On the airwaves in the plush lobbies comes a familiar song as I make my way through the crowd, and love becomes a stranger who beckons me on. The song, the voice, and the promise match one another, and they are seductive. They send me reeling into their cinerama of glamorous women and granite men and down some bare airport existential walkway. I am going down in search of something unknown. What abysmal truth awaits? What danger? Is there love in the end?

Then, after the movie, I retreat into the cold. The big city's remnant lights give way to the darkness of farmlands on both sides. The burning promise and fantasy subside in the dark night of the soul. But thoughts gradually return again to my real town, to real people in real time, and to the promise we are really given.

26

Nein!

I said to my soul, be still, and let the dark come upon you

FROM THE COLLEGE LIBRARY window looking down I see a woman and a man cross paths. There is buoyant laughter and wild gesticulating as they slow down but continue to walk. The I and Thou is only in passing, and their possible I and It objectifications as they continue their walk are not necessarily negative in tone. Had there been a stiff politeness or angry words, the I and It transcendence may have taken the form of a freedom-from, a sigh of relief, in the walking away.

The theologian Karl Rahner speaks of transcendence as a flight from the world, a relinquishment of its provisional and ungrounded goods and values. It opposes the temptation to eat, drink, and be merry, or as in the current fad, eat, pray, and love, and thus to round oneself off in this world. Eastern mysticism is well known also for its renunciation of desire. The Western medieval mysticism of the dark night of the soul, namely a withdrawal of the senses from the stimulations of the world, is also what lies behind T. S. Eliot's lines in *The Four Quartets*. I said to my soul, be still, and let the dark come upon you, which will be the darkness of God. Wait without hope, continues Eliot, for hope would be hope for the wrong thing. Wait without love, for love would be love for the wrong thing. At the end of this passage it is the darkness that becomes the light, and the stillness the dancing. It is in flight-from, as in repulsion from fire or snake, that ironically we draw close to Truth and Life in the big sense.

Nein!

It seems such a short time ago that I came to the seminary in San Anselmo and met Bill, who lifted weights in the basement, whose room was at the end of the hallway, and who had books by Karl Barth. He told me of how Barth had started the current boom in theological studies, but that I would have to wait till my senior year to study Barth. I resolved that some day I too would be mature enough to read and learn the religious secret behind Barth's theology. I have now indeed read Barth and have learned that his signal achievement was exactly his own monumentally articulated revolt against the wrong hopes and wrong loves of all flesh, and the powers and principalities of this world.

Well-known by now is that black day in August, 1914, that sparked Barth's revolution. That day almost all the theological teachers Barth had venerated joined with many other German intellectuals to issue a proclamation in support of the war policies of Wilhelm II and the German government. Barth was only twenty-nine, and he was outraged. He and his teachers must have heard the speech of the Crown Prince of the German empire inciting the people to arms, declaring that Germany must protect itself from attack. The very existence of empire is at stake! Every delay would be a treachery to the Fatherland.

The Crown Prince was also the man who had written *Germany in Arms* one year earlier. What can be fairer, said the book, than to see steel helmets glitter in the sunshine, the galloping exercises, and the ride to the attack! Yet there is something fairer. The coming life and death struggle on behalf of our country!

It was all lies. The whole world knew that Russia was hardly planning an attack on Germany, that the accusation that a French aviator had dropped bombs on Nurenberg was entirely baseless, and that Germany's claim that its actions were purely defensive and that "not one human being among us had dreamed of war" was absurd. What Barth's theological teachers did in letting philosophy supplant and suppress theology, and in supporting Germany's ultimata to Russia and then to France and Belgium, could and should be for any thoughtful pilgrim a writing on the wall, a sign of the bankruptcy of nineteenth century liberal spirituality and theology. It is one thing to seek to interpret religion and theology in the light of the intuitions and feelings of the human race broadly, and quite another to dissolve the truth and power of particular religions and their unique history and theology in philosophical generalities. Should not philosophy approach theology with some respect? Should not the assumption be that theology, grounded in its own history and scriptures, may have something important to say, and that we as philosophers are willing to listen?

Barth perceived correctly that a church can become so narrowly enamored with its own cultural philosophy and so enthralled by the secular drift of its own times that it renders itself impotent to stand in judgment, in transcendence, over against the poisoning of its own mind.

Actually, the world for young Barth was one fat lie as far as the eye could see. From his pinnacle of prayer and pulpit in the Swiss Reformed Church in Safenwil he was prepared to say Nein! not just to the war propaganda, the liberal theology that supported it, and the cozy accommodation of the church to the bourgeois culture. The German empire marching headstrong to claim its place in the sun became a prism through which the many-faceted wretchedness of the human condition itself came into sharp relief.

Barth's metaphysical thunderstorm propelled itself forward by its exposure of the prolific Babylonian corruption on the ground. Our life comes to a screeching, shattering halt in the face of the divine No! to the old being that we are and to the free erotic course of unrighteousness upon which we are embarked. But this all-embracing No! catapults us to the divine Yes!, to the new being that we can be. The door is flung wide open to our citizenship in heaven, to the life beyond this life, to an invisible point of observation, the watchtower of Habukkuk. The invisible point of *Nein!* intervenes in our closed-rounded life in this world, and the mysterious possibility emerges, says Barth, of our regarding ourselves as objects not identical with ourselves.

Leaving aside the fact that an object's not being identical with itself is hardly a mysterious possibility but rather a conceptual impossibility in the plainest of views, it is Barth's asseverations about the unbearability of Babylon and his robust account of the necessity of renunciation, the invisible tower of Habukkuk, that marks him as a profound soul from whom we truly have a lot to learn. We will wait without hope if it be hope for the wrong thing. We will wait without love if it be love for the wrong thing.

The days of wine and roses again conspire to divert me with one entertainment after another from community, creative work, and excellence in the leadership of worship. Immediate gratifications take precedence over long term goals, short-term concerns for my own survival over solidarity with the earth and its creatures. Shame on us when we objectify and dehumanize sentient beings. Nothing is more decadent or vulgar than to usurp the sacred soil of I and Thou. Woe to us who prioritize profit over justice, and woe to those who are complicit in such wrongdoing. I read that 60 million people in India now boast a standard of living equal to the most technologically advanced societies of the world, while 900 million still live in poverty. I am too comfortable and smug in my own fair community, sheltered from the hunger and violence of refugee camps and slums and their starving animals, and even from the drug gangs and crime rings of our own big cities.

Save me from complacency and complicity. Save me from false loves and fraudulent hopes, and from a cold, cold heart.

Prayer and preaching are indeed a bulwark, a mountain of retreat. But Barth would never acknowledge kindly those immersed in literature, music, art, philosophy, and science as fellow participants in logos. Cannot theirs too be a yoga whereby they know darknesses equal to the dark night of the soul, and theirs be heights that look eye to eye upon the Nein! pulpit of Pastor Barth? Cannot theirs be a fortress as invincible to the arrows of decadence as the tower of Habukkuk?

The tower of Nein! will never become for us a permanent place in the sun. The smiling valley and rolling river call to us from across the wide Missouri. We have promises to keep, pebbles to return to the beach. The tower cannot but be a temporary retreat from the world, a time to be silent and think, an observation outpost where on behalf of the world below we watch for signs on the horizon of poachers, of the dreaded black-robed Janjaweed in Darfur, of the soldiers of Herod.

I cannot come and reside with you in the tower, Pastor Barth. I do not do well when I am sealed off from the world psychically. I would miss the Bulldog Cafe and the companionship of women and men at lunch, especially the old man they used to call Big Paul Hoffman and who speaks of still having the volumes of Schaff's history of the church. There are new CDs that interest me. I want to listen to John Adams' *The Dharma at Big Sur* again. Music is evolving so athletically now, Pastor Barth. It is both East and West at the same time and includes inflections by the tabla and the sitar. I want you to hear the new interpretations of ancient and austere sacred music. And I enjoy the soccer and track meets here. Some evenings ago I tried to write, but there was no resisting the final call for the boys' 100 meter dash over the loudspeaker.

I watched the boys' 1600 meter run too. The boy in the front was a bit stocky and I knew he would tire. The boy running second was trying too hard. It was the boy running third who looked strong and wiry, and his face was free of strain and worry, as if he knew something that no one else did. It was he who easily won the race. It was dark and the stadium lights were bright when I heard everyone screaming for their loved ones during the girls' 1600 meter run and the final relays. Go, go, go, go go, Sarah, yelled one older woman close to me over and over again hoarsely in a heavy, contralto voice. It was a pathetic drone, almost a wail, as if she was dying. She was giving everything she had.

27

The Tower

To which dost thou belong? Spirit or nature?

LONELY IN OUR TOWERS of transcendence and hearing the whoosh and whisper of the wind in the pines, we must return home, back to I and Thou ground where our loved ones wait and the sheep graze and the coyotes and the purple sage call. The ramparts of Habukkuk could not be the final and permanent resting place for our souls when they felt so remote, and when there were crossroads to be reckoned with, rivers to be crossed, unfinished business to bring to a close, and much more to be learned down below.

In school we learned how to think, in places of worship we were fed the premium food of missionaries and pilgrims on their sacred journeys. The acquired gifts of school and religion, however, are to be taken into the world to serve wayward lives searching for a passage or foothold, to protect ecosystems and wildlife sanctuaries, to become saints and prophets hammering out justice, ringing out freedom, singing songs of love, exhaling the lofty thoughts that ennoble and illumine life's little day. How can it be said that these natural virtues of good will and originality and talent, and the determination to know and create, all partake of corruptibility and only expose the vitality of our sin? There is iniquity, no doubt, but does it nullify all our thoughts, all our work, as far as the eye can see?

What is more, in the negative tower of Habakkuk Barth could not countenance Sin as a cobra scaling the fortress and hiding in the rocks of that high and holy place. In the mountainous abode of the person of heaven with the power of prayer, Sin allegedly has no light even to survive, no air to breathe, no space to maneuver anywhere on the transcendence-immanence axis. The new being of heaven is the old being of dust ignited, transformed, and liberated by the lightning of God.

Nor was Barth aware of the scourge of the person of heaven, that it is not easy for a person to transcend the sidereal place itself to which she or he has already ascended. Transcendence of a second order is critical if we are to stay honest with ourselves in the tower. To survey the bright valleys and amber fields and shining cities of Babylon is easier than to peer into the dark ravines of one's own soul, where hide Wrath, Lust, Pride, and Greed even at that high invisible place. Barth does not know that there is a stain on the new being's white robes. Those white Sunday morning robes of Truth and Justice and Holiness and Goodness not only convey divinity but hide desperate guilts and fears, lusts and strivings, cheap egoisms, half-truths. I know this not only within my own self, but it has happened and is happening around me as a professional pastor. Barth does not see the shadow of Death fall across the outpost itself.

The Buzzard circles overhead. The lonely tower is blindsided by the energy and ecstasy of its momentous breakthrough. Its pride, its participation in its own partiality and relativity, its own conjurings of dancing girls, as by the third and fourth century desert fathers, are denied and unaccounted for. The fateful hand from the gutter pulls at the hem of heaven's garment, dragging it below the pale of immanence.

Heaven and earth are connected. Scattered are the proud in the imagination of their hearts. The mighty are brought down from their thrones and towers.

It is not as though Barth completely misunderstood the nineteenth century liberal theologians against whom he revolted. He had in fact learned just from them of the polar oppositions of principle and passion, worship and world, essence and existence. Religion breaks us into two halves, he said, spirit and nature, spirit that delights in the word of God, nature that is swayed by an opposite kind of energy. To which dost thou belong? Who art thou? We are forced into choosing both because we cannot choose one or the other exclusively. The more thou dost endeavor to synthesize the two, the more their oppositional tension is manifest. It comes as something of a surprise to me that Barth saw this so clearly.

But Barth is just mocking us, and he is scoffing at the nineteenth century conquering heroes. It was in particular Friedrich Schleiermacher who, in his important second speech in the book addressed to the cultured despisers of religion, had defended the religious life as the sacred and creative embrace of reason and the world, and he had described that union in turn as a romance between agency and receptivity, with all its sexual tension. Why does this deserve to be mocked, Pastor Barth? Can you not bear this tension? You come to the brink of Truth and turn away in derision.

As the agent of heaven we lie on the bosom of the receptive world. At the creative moment the world is our body and we are its soul, its thinking and deciding. We are the mind that creates, and at the same time we are the receptive person of dust and our lover is heaven itself. The Flight into Egypt, for example, is the form we receive, and we bang out chords, draw figures on the canvas, or write sentences to realize the form. We receive, we act. A marriage occurs between matter and meaning, ear and essence, eye and idea, feeling and form. Beauty is born.

Receptivity is grace, agency is the liturgy we practice, the cross we bear. Receptivity and agency yield to one another. Goodness is born. The Word is made flesh.

A state of equilibrium wherein the mind that acts and the person who receives did not stimulate the other would not represent life and all its existentia. Schleiermacher expressed the migrant power of transcendence, if not the nausea of its original drive, as the figure of the vanishing maiden and the eyes of her forlorn lover. He also knew the tug and gestalt of the aching heart. The feeling overspreads your whole being, as the blush of shame and love over the face of the maiden. Schleiermacher was not driven away, as was Barth, from the collision and the collusion, the flight-from and the erotic pull, the distance and the desire, in the mystical dance of love and the mythical drama of life.

28

The Uncompahgre
Please come back to a heart that is true

My life as a partially retired part-time pastor of a small church in this rural college town has worked reasonably well so far. I walk or bicycle almost everywhere, I eat fresh, natural, gluten-free foods, and cook curried dishes for myself. I am a partial vegan. I am not a purist anything. I have time to teach a philosophy class and write these thoughts in the college library, and at the same time to remain responsibly engaged with the local community. In my older years I have become something of a muse.

But the spiritual quandary persists. How live justly, frugally, and reverently in a proud and prosperous society? How give up my reliance on fossil fuels when it is so cold in the winter and so hot in the summer, and where there is no effective public transportation? How live in such a congenial and sheltered place and yet in solidarity with beings injured or displaced by the traumas of our time? Will I ever return the pebbles to the seashore of Maine? The questions embarrass me. I wonder if my guilt is disproportionate with the facts.

When the work of my week is done I face the prison of being alone. The dark emptiness of the house stares back at me with alligator eyes. It is a force of existence against which I am not strong, but feeble. I am an easy prey, though sometimes I do withstand the pestilence of demons. In the Snake's mouth the soul flops convulsively. In Kurukshetra the warfare is asymmetric.

And in Kurukshetra my Quaker avatar is my best defense, who I continue to see in the city. She serves me blueberry tea, which I mix with

The Uncompahgre

black tea. We start and close with silence. She lives in a solar-powered home built by her husband, and she cultivates a native plant garden in the yard. Abutting this naturalistic corporeal world is her mythical world of silence and spirit, which she has long ceased to try and explain. She is very intelligent and articulate and worldly-wise and can speak of movies, mainstream books, natural foods, and even the nightclub Margarita's, where she has gone dancing herself. The center of gravity lies, however, in the other world. She is humble and has admitted lately that she is learning from me too. She is not an activist, she says, but a contemplative. I have been seeing her for ten years.

In the heart's Hall of Dreams, I still see Dr. DNA step out after work on Tuesdays and Thursdays into the starry, starry night. He stops as usual at the creek where the road turns and he stands on the wooden bridge that leads into the park. Tonight the wind is blowing from the south. It is coming from the Gulf, he thinks, where the oil from the leak continues to bellow out under pressure at the bottom of the sea at over ten or twenty times times the rate per day as were the oil company's estimates. It has now spread onto the coastline, and over five hundred birds, over two hundred rare sea turtles, and over thirty mammals have been found dead so far. He does not want to think further about that. His doubts and premonitions are troubling. They have already darkened his mind and produced restless nights. His former wife would suggest resuming his medication, but he has held out thus far. The long and strenuous walk, the running water in the creek, and the sound of the wind in the big cedars and cottonwoods do more to ease the astringency in his soul than the medication.

But tonight he hears through the water and the wind an otherworldly sound coming from the direction of the sea, and he lingers and listens. Deep is calling to deep. A large orchestra is playing the flapping, nesting, chasing sounds of birds in the spring's early morning hours. The swarming, unpredictable notes are metaphors of life, of love requited, love spurned, taut uncertainties, avid anticipations, savage jealousies and suspicions, the joys of families and children, irrepressible laughter, the wet handkerchiefs as the train leaves the station. But the rites of spring grow hushed in the echoes of the Deepwater Horizon's massive explosion fifty miles out in the Gulf beyond the mist. The ominous sound is all in all, a night that has fallen before night.

A fishermen's chorus on the seashore sings, with strumming guitars, Forsaken is the name of this hallowed world, Wrecked the name of our livelihood. The ballad of a fisherman's wife is tender and shaky, and her voice breaks with, What life can be in such a black sea? Dr. DNA has never heard the term barrier island or the names Grand Isle, Breton Sound, Chandeleur Sound, Barataria Bay, Delta Wildlife Refuge, Grand Bayou. The names of these sacred places are unveiled to the world in the opera that follows between the fishermen, the unseen oil company's defensive tenor heard from beyond the mist in the Gulf, and the aggravated, political presence of Barack Obama, hoping to provide a ballast to the nation and intoning the proper role of government, the demands of justice, and the call for the restoration of the gulf and its marshes.

"Swift to its close ebbs out life's little day./ Earth's joys grow dim, its glories pass away." Those lines from the hymn *Abide with Me* come from a small church on the blue waters and the green coast. They cast their soft glow in the hamlet at the close of day, but they are set against the backdrop of streaks of red and smudges of black on the sea. A nightmarish blue and red light, as from a police car in a city noir, flashes in Dr. DNA's imagination, what with more and more square miles of wetlands eroded every year as a result of dredging by oil companies and poisons from upstream. The music whose opening bars sounded out the loud and happy bird-swarming morning hours, that was then tragically interrupted by the frightening booms from fifty miles away in the gulf, and that continued with the voices of the fishermen, the oil company's tenor, and the Barack Obama government, now continues with a melancholy closing movement at eventide with lyrical, rhythmic, and melodic variations of the hymn.

There is life at the bottom of the sea. It is Dr. DNA's own refrain as he stands on the wooden bridge over the stream and meditates upon the mystery of the sea. A saxophone in a jazz ensemble on Bourbon Street wails out the blues amid the tinkling of glasses to continue the Earth Requiem. The sturdy dirge-like singing of the chorale, the large orchestra suffused and undergirded by the organ, has a distinct contemporary feel. It is both sacred and profane. It is manic and stark, at times with noisy gongs and clanging cymbals evoking the ingenuity and madness of humanity in the twenty-first century. It is also a sarabande and vesperish and bluesy, with variations of the dusky singing emanating from the church intermeshed with the floating, unbroken lyricism of the saxophone.

"Change and decay in all around I see." That line gives way to the eternal and universal Thou, but the Thou is not unchanging, as in the old hymn. The Thou is rather the mystery, hardly comprehended by his scientific

The Uncompahgre

colleagues, of the million moving parts of the Regenerative Process. The voice of the Thou, far from being substance for test tubes and laboratories, is rather the music Dr.DNA hears, and it is dense with prophetic meaning and apocalyptic of the looming tragedy of the twenty-first century. We search for the face but not the deep. We lust with our eyes but comprehend not with our hearts. Few know that lovers have feelings, landscapes have lairs, and there is life at the bottom of the sea. It is the hymn that gives the music girth and depth and memory. It is its message that gives the music its comfort and hope and truth. The lines are enhanced percussively at times by tabla and drums and military-style trumpets, recalling how the hymn is played by the Indian army on Independence Day in commemoration of Gandhi. It was Gandhi's favorite hymn.

It is here, pilgrim friends, that we must leave Dr. DNA standing on the wooden bridge leading into the park, though not without just a tinge of sadness. But we will not worry about him. He will get some sleep tonight, having heard the music in the water and the wind. I must continue my story from where we left off, the scene shifting now to a high desert valley in the Rocky Mountains. Batman, the black cat who had adopted me and I him in Seattle, was with me.

I was fortunate to find an accredited pastoral counselor in a nearby resort town higher up in the mountains. I began seeing him regularly. The small house that I bought had a woodburning stove and I started chopping my own wood. It was in this town that I began walking to church, the post office, the bank, and the grocery store. Something in me said that this was finally the right and healthy way to live. It was a brand new chapter in my life and I would take advantage of it. Perhaps it was the voice of Luke, my counselor in Seattle, who had emphasized health as the highest priority.

The San Juan range rose to the south, the Grand Mesa to the east, the Uncompahgre Plateau stretched across the west, and the Uncompahgre River flowed through the valley. I planted black currant seedlings and other native shrubs in the yard. The skies were blue, the yellow-shafted flicker came to the yard in the summer, the women offered me rides in the rain, and I lifted my eyes to the hills and was happy. But my new life in Paradise was fragmentary and short-lived, as it had been in the Garden of the Knowledge of Good and Evil near the sea, as it had been in the plush town on the Appalachian Trail in the Berkshire hills, and as it always has been and always will be.

The Meaning of These Days

There was, however, one critical difference about this Paradise. This time I had learned my lesson. This time I would not give up my power. I would not yield to the alluring claims of the woman, who said, Let us play today. Tomorrow we can go for dinner to the new Italian restaurant on Highway 50, visit the Black Canyon to look down and watch the eagles fly and the river far below, or drive south on the scenic blue highway winding toward the majestic San Juans.

My Nein! was not cerebral. It was thunder and lightning upon the deep in the soul. Neither of us compromised. In one way I had the advantage. I was older and had had experience with the game. Furthermore, she was so much like me, I thought. I could read her so well. She, on the other hand, had immense powers of her own, her youthful energy, natural good looks, and feminine charm.

I spent time with the counselor seeking help again and again with the burning in my soul. Once again I was shaken at the foundations. Dripping icicles hung like ornaments on his porch in the winter. The seasons went by and he took notes on his yellow pad. I was lovesick, and he was quiet. He did not know what to say out loud. I knew what he was thinking, but I did not believe it. He was thinking, Find another woman. This one does not love you. The silence bounded off the mountains, which shot up steeply to the sky all around.

The wind is rhapsodic in this landscape of looming monuments of red rock, purple sage, Gambel oak, service berry, and groves of fir, ponderosa pine, cottonwoods, dwarf pines, cedars, and aspens. Driving back on the winding road you pass meadows with No Hunting signs and gathered elk, briar patches and thickets, and the river on the left brings you the only comfort you know. You pull over just to gaze and listen. This I call prayer. Tumbleweeds cross the highway to rest against fences and barns. Whatever happened to the lynx that the Bureau of Land Management had reintroduced in these mountains from Canada? Have they survived against the coyotes and the cougars? How can I leave these vast spaces where the deer and the antelope play?

Country music and cowboys and cowgirls were the dominant culture in the towns, but a cultish kind of New Age spirituality had established a foothold in our church. Walking high at Owl Creek Pass among spruce and cotoneaster with red berries in the spring, the leader of the group dismissed Locke, Berkeley, Hume, Freud, and the whole history of Western thought as if he were smashing back ping-pong balls. His was some anemic and hasty version of Vedanta, and he reminded me of the transparent blue and blank-eyed Dr. Manhattan in the movies, reconstructed after a physics accident out of atomic fibers and incapable of making love or rising and falling with the waves of human emotion. The consistently arrogant tone week after week weighed upon me, and I discussed the man and the group with my counselor.

The guitar solo of another man who came for the services for his mother was of a piece with the austere beauty of the high desert valley. At graveside among the cedars he kneeled on the ground in the middle of the circle and played *Red River Valley* meticulously, broodingly, ruefully. His gaze was earthward and inward, as if nothing else mattered. Nothing else did matter, yet now everything was endurable. I had come all this way just to hear that enchanted campfire song played so lovingly. It was all worth it, the heartaches, the indignities, the failures. I have heard many renditions of the song since I was a boy in the Himalayan Christian missionary schools, but its immaculate realization in a hillside cemetery that day was as unsentimental as it was rapturous, like the river.

"Please come back to a heart that is true." Does this agony of the heart have an answer? Yes, O monks. Let the Red River be the mythical river that flows through the valley of our days, sharing with us the nurture of its own fresh Truth. The experience of the sacred river is different in different traditions, though there are often gardens there, and trees with leaves for the healing of the nations. When love is broken, or when a dear one dies, someone goes and sits by the river and weeps. The people in the valley know that there is healing in the sounds of the river and in the shimmering points of light in the water, and they gather there with the saints and lay down their burdens, which the river carries away.

29

Blue Oaks
I myself arrive in the valley of dry bones

In California I bought a bicycle and helmet for the three mile ride to the church. The commercial development juggernaut was crawling up from the big city, and these would be the last years for open fields and the big old trees with screeching eagles and their nests. The For Sale signs might well have said, The End Is Near. I would pick up the mail in the small town and make my way up the hill through the translucent haze of blue oaks to the attractive church. At one time the forests of this lovely tree were abundant up and down the Sierra Nevada foothills. Long ago the over one thousand square miles of delta to the west and south near what is now the big city were a rich tidal marsh area with an abundance of bear, deer, cranes, ducks, and swans. Sycamores and thickets thrived along the rivers.

On my bicycle rides I was aware of a creepy frontier feeling of viperiousness. Dogs and cats were in danger because of coyotes. A car full of men pulled up early on a Sunday morning in the fog and I was asked for directions. Good that I was at the entrance to the town and it was residential on both sides. I pointed to the light at the other end of town, a right at which would lead out to the freeway. There was a tense pause and the car moved on.

The church also felt sinister right from the start. There was the matter of the interim minister's unofficial assistant who wanted my job, had a small following in the church, continued his membership there for a while even after I came, and then left with his flock to try and start a new church. Furthermore, two of the church's main leaders seemed hostile to my success from the beginning. A group that adversarialized my leadership quickly formed around them. Nothing I brought, no sermon, no musical or liturgical or theological idea, no pastoral or educational or outreach initiative, no gesture of reconciliation, won me favor with this entrenched group. What few strengths I had seemed to grate against and threaten these powers of the church, and the well was thoroughly poisoned. I learned that what was supposed to be a trusted place of nourishment had actually been contaminated long before I came.

I was hurt and my temperature had risen. The question, Can these bones live? which I applied to myself, stalked me in the valley of dry bones. Never had I been treated with so much negativity, never seen so much clinging to power, never known so much wrath and spiritual carnage.

I brought two weapons to the confrontation that loomed. The bicycle ride bespoke a certain scrappiness I brought to this embattled ministry, and it preserved within me a modicum of dignity and poise. At least my intentions were good, trying to do the right thing and live a healthy lifestyle in the face of what was looking increasingly like the scene of dry bones strewn in the valley, a defeat to go down in history. The other weapon was the unique avatar of Reason I was able to find in the big city, a pastoral counselor whose own staunchness more than matched what I was up against.

The pastoral counselor was in fact the supervisor of a Clinical Pastoral Education program in a large hospital. Since I had myself availed of exactly this program in Atlanta, my level of respect for this man was already high. He was blind, and his tiny office was made smaller by the general clutter and the special machine by which he could read articles and reports. The adjoining office on one side was separated only by a door through which I could hear voices easily. I was always uneasy about being heard in that other room and spoke softly. Fortunately, the corridor was always loud and busy and it must have helped drown out my voice for anyone eavesdropping.

The counselor listened to me with bent head and closed eyes, as if he was asleep. He was never asleep. From the start he wanted to know why I was giving away my power. The question hit me between the eyes, and it led to my own inner self-probing. Was I so vainglorious that I was in denial? How had the counselor picked up on this so quickly? Was I a weakling, one who always gives away one's power?

I knew what it meant to give away power. It had happened with both my first and my second wife, though in both cases I had belatedly retrieved it. Had I been a slut? Is not the giving away of one's power the giving away of one's soul? What had I gotten in each case in exchange for my power? What was I getting now? Was my scrappiness a true defense or self-deception? To what extent was I an accurate judge of my own feelings? How forthright was I being with the counselor about the real depth of my insecurity? This last question was an especially painful one for me, and I gave myself some credit for surfacing it.

Was there in fact a basis for the antagonism of that group in the church? Had I been inept with the youth? Were my relations with the young families strained? Working with youth had never been my strength. I needed my counselor's affirmation, but praise did not come easily to his lips. I knew by my own experience in Clinical Pastoral Education that undeserved support can be detrimental therapeutically. Instead, he had a way of zooming in on my vulnerabilities, and I squirmed under his steady gaze. There were times I tried to diffuse the intensity inside that small office. Once I came armed with Edward Farley's award-winning *Divine Empathy*, but he grew impatient with the reading I did about the human tendency to absolutize finite goods and maintain postures of certainty and patriotism.

No, Pilgrim, the blind man would not listen to my braggadocio and the commentary on idolatry, the roots of evil, and the human desire to secure one's life against tragedy. He returned me to the question that pursued me in the valley of dry bones. Why was I so afraid? He wanted me to look those church leaders straight in the eyes and reason with them. Why, he himself tangles with the hospital administrators on budget issues. He himself faces down extreme-minded chaplaincy students.

It was hard to open up and try to explain that this was hardly a cerebral matter, that it was as plain as day that I was unwanted and ganged up against, that in any case I was not as good with words as he was, and that there were already ongoing meetings about me that were organized and led by members of the hostile group. It was kin to the ancient shame that my father had felt when called upon to describe what had happened between him and my mother. It was a shame no one in my extended family could ever talk about, not my uncles or aunts, not my cousins or in-laws.

The church and I parted company cordially. I gave those adversarial leaders hugs and they gave me hugs. I preached affirming sermons to the end. But that was my public face. I was bruised and steaming underneath. Yet there was something undeniably redemptive about my time there. Redemption has a million moving parts. It was partly in the friendships I had made, which would outlive the battles lost and won. I have continued to visit quite regularly with some of those persons over the years.

Redemption was also in what took place in the blind man's office. Though he was blind, his darkness was in fact the great red sea of eastern clouds at dawn. Between his classes he had walked me through my ordeal step by step without becoming submerged in it himself. He had believed in me. He had tried to teach me to box. He could see that I was not a good boxer, that I cut and ran when the going was rough. In adverse social settings I was not self-assertive. I was the skinny kid on the beach who the big muscular guy Atlas pushed out of the way, and all the girls adored him.

There were times I expressed the naked truth about my brokenness, masked by a lifetime of cultivated appearances. I could see him soften momentarily, and he would step back. But it was the part about power to which our conversations returned directly or indirectly. He was naïve and dead wrong about how effective reasoning with the leaders of that church would be. But he expected me to assert my power regardless, and not to run. He expected me to reclaim the power I had given away and to maintain my power no matter what. And he tried, like a good coach, to teach me how to carry through on these things.

The voices of that church echo, its faces pass by, in the land of dreams. Still three-dimensional are the sanctuary rafters toward which I twirled coins when I was alone. The leaves I watched in the fall go round and round in a whirlwind in the courtyard when I wrote my sermons whirl today at the back of my mind, and the thin cat, for whose life I lived in fear because of the coyotes, comes and curls up in my lap. The friends who were helpless against what was happening but had me over in their homes for dinner are among the people I hold close at the end of the day.

To the blind counselor I say Thank You to conclude this chapter. Stepping on the scales, if I mistake not, you and I were perhaps similar in intelligence and education and age, but you were a strong and versatile boxer, a champion with no losses.

30

Buffalo Rock
I do best when I'm not alone

THE MAIN BRIDGE ACROSS the Red River, which separates Fargo, North Dakota, from Moorhead, Minnesota, was my bridge to the twenty-first century. I married a German man and an American woman, an opera star in Germany, at midnight on New Year's Eve, 2000. In the summer I bicycled along the river on one side and a carpet of flowers on the other, and then across a narrow footbridge into Moorhead, where I served as an interim minister. Batman and I had an apartment in Fargo. In the frigid winter, even when it was twenty or so degrees below freezing, I caught the bus to the Fargo bus depot and walked across the railway tracks and then across the main bridge and through a residential area to the church. On the way back I followed the same route. At Atomic Coffee near the railroad tracks in Moorhead I introduced some fellow pilgrims to survivor's tea. I wrapped the expensive teabag, used lightly, in wax paper and kept it for later use. Today I would use the term existential tea.

From the bus depot I saw the east-west trains go by and heard the various buses called out, and I recalled the Greyhound bus depot in San Francisco. It felt like only yesterday when the ship sailed under the Golden Gate Bridge. The railroad tracks had the feel and smell of growing up near the railway station in Ferozepore, with some empty trains left standing for good. Sitting there you could brood upon the transience and delicateness and perpetual perishing of beings, until your bus was called. All flesh is grass. The grass withers, the sleek, colossal steam engines and their whistles give way to the electric engines and their diabolical drones, and the passenger trains yield to the double-stack two-mile long monster I-It trains with no soul at all. There are not even hobos here, no families, no crowds or red-coated coolies or *chai wallas* on the platform waiting. Many of the trains do not even stop.

What if there were passenger trains instead of freight trains coming and going constantly? What if our economies did not separate us so? Our towns would have thriving marketplaces with jobs, livable communities, viable schools, a depth of existence, a chance to love, instead of the striving for silver and gold, and the brief and brutish passing of one's existence from job to job, garrison to garrison. What if in 1955 the Eisenhower administration had thought more of the human factor instead of the military and industry factor, and started building up the passenger train system instead of the freeway system, which has carved up our wild lands and played havoc with wildlife migration patterns? Had they done this, they would have helped nurture the soul of America, which is where our true strength lies as a nation. It can hardly lie in our military might, which corrupts our powers of observation. It does not lie in our prosperity, which fattens us and enfeebles us at the core.

No, the only sign of life you will see on these tracks is the graffiti on the sides of the double-stack cars passing by. Squiggled by anonymous, invisible, apocalyptic figures under the cover of darkness, they signify the only will to live on this line. In code the figures assert themselves and convey who they are. They are the Underground, and their language and art a sign of flesh and blood, with their cryptic meanings and manifestos smeared on the cars for the world to see. Contrast them with the noisy, heavy, rust-colored steel-on-steel behemoths on which the language is written, and the often protruding products of multinational companies pulled by economic engines that are oblivious, on their way to their terminals in the big cities, of the little towns and the people in them, let alone of the wildlife habitats through which they travel, the streams and rivers fed by the snows of the Rockies and the Sierra Nevada and the Cascades, and the farm fields that were once prairies, the breeding grounds of countless species of birds and ground animals, including the American buffalo, many of which have been long extinct.

Decipher the writing of the dark figures no one sees, pilgrim readers. Look there and you can read, We are the French Resistance. We resist occupying armies, the Nazi, the Israeli, the Soviet, the American. We are the writers, the artists, and the film-makers who expose the power and the greed of corporations and empires. We are the New Existentialists who say, Freedom before Order, Justice before Peace. We are the Buddhist monks arrested for marching for freedom in Burma and Tibet and now languish in prisons dark. We are the ones who rallied in Iran against the clergy oppressors and their Revolutionary Guard. We have been tortured, and we too grow pale in prisons dark. We are the Underground.

On the next car we have: We are the undocumented. We are the boat people. We are the voices of the refugees of Palestine, of Darfur, of Rwanda, of Haiti. We are the *Dalits*, the Suppressed Ones, the Broken Ones. Some of us flee the prejudice and violence and poverty in our countries, which have long ceased to sustain our families. We have lost our livelihoods, so in desperation we buy false papers, risk the border guards, and cross the desert to earn money to send to our mothers, fathers, spouses, and children. If they catch us, we shall return. Among us we count the addicts, some of whom confess that life is out of control, that they are naked in the face of their own hard-wired brains. They live one day at a time, and they pray every night to a Higher Power to keep them clean. We are all the Underground.

And look over there. We are the Dark Mountain Project. We are the people of Deep Ecology, believers in the I and Thou primal ground, not in a culture of industrial abatoirs, not in a for-profit economy which makes objects of everything there is, not in shallow capitalist fixes which return us to corporate colonialism. We are the braves that return when all are asleep to visit our sacred murmuring rivers, our once undefiled valleys. We are the dead of Wounded Knee come to frolic again, and hunt and fish again, in the meadows and by the flowing streams at the foot of the mountains, and to pick out the place where the village was, and where the horses grazed. We are the soldiers separated from the rolling river and the smiling valley across the wide Missouri for seven long years. We are the Underground.

We are the kidnapped children, abused and exploited. We write the cries of our hearts on the sides of the trains for our mothers far away. Some day they will see the train go by, and they will read and know that we still love them and cry for them. Some day someone will write music for our words, and then people will perhaps comprehend the loneliness of the world. We are the Underground.

We are the homeless. We sleep in the dark hidden corners of parking lots even in the winter. Around us are busy streets with billboards and neon lights, parked cars, parking meters, high-rise towers, dance clubs, buildings in disuse and protected by iron gates, roped off spaces, food vendors, and police vehicles at the gas station. There is a noisy swell of people from the stadium when the game is over, and when the workday is done fashionable people with bags or briefcases hurry on foot to the subways. Couples from apartments go by with a dog. There are no cats in the alleys or other ground animals. Some of us have shopping carts in which we keep our belongings. We stand, some of us, on the sides of the streets and ask for change. We are the Underground.

Such were my thoughts as I sat in the Fargo bus depot waiting for my bus and watching the trains go by. A retired elderly but energetic medical doctor noted the lament in my sermons and prayers about the destruction of forests, prairies, and wetlands. The Red River is a grassland area. The deciduous forests of upper Wisconsin and upper Michigan begin not too far to the east. The doctor himself referred to the plowing under of the wild grasses as we drove at his insistence to a prairie preserve in the spring. See that enormous rock outcropping in the distance? he asked as we stood at the prairie's edge. That's Buffalo Rock.

A hard-driving fellow of intelligence, he was older and not much bigger than me, but he played indoor tennis all winter. I followed him as he thrashed through the tall deep-tufted bluestem, switch grass, goldenrod, and thistle toward Buffalo Rock. Later we also stopped at a stream with swampy woods, the Jurassic limbs of trees reaching across from both sides. Mosquitoes hummed around us, but I had on hat and gloves and layers of clothing. The trees next to the stream cannot be cut, explained the doctor.

I moved on later that year to my last full-time settled pastorate, also in the midwest. It was my daily walk to the university library that kept me braced there for all that happened. Not being able to find a suitable pastoral counselor, I was fortunate to find a helpful and open-minded spiritual director. It was she of whom I spoke earlier, who emphasized that my study, walking, and other mundane and routine activities can be approached as spiritual disciplines, forms of prayer, yogas. The manifold and relentless demands of this new congregation were debilitating in the long term, and I was glad to have a personal life of reading and writing, walking and bicycling. Friendships with two graduate student women came to a screeching halt and left their scars.

Batman was overcome with diabetes. In the end he needed the comfort of sitting close to me on the arm rest of my big orange chair. He had been my companion for over ten years. I held him in a blanket when he was euthanized, and I wept.

The Meaning of These Days

In the wake of the attacks of September 11, 2001, our area pastors talked about the military build-up in the Persian Gulf area and then the invasion of Iraq itself. We were alarmed by the unilateralism and the Bring 'em on swagger of George W. Bush and his administration. Fires were burning across the nation and world, and creeping fear weighed heavy on journalists and politicians and unsympathetic persons in federal employ. There were hard-charging activists among us who were already known for their impassioned letters to the newspaper on justice concerns and who served unstintingly on boards across the city. Now they became even busier self-delegated spokespersons for us and tried to mobilize Ninevah for peace vigils and prayer meetings. All of this, of course, over and above keeping up with their personal and family life, continuing education, various church meetings, pastoral calling, administration, and bulletin and sermon preparations.

It was impossible to do all these things well. Even though I shared their outrage against the policies of the new administration, in my private thoughts I questioned their obsessiveness, and along with that their standards. I wondered about the carcinogenicity of, and behind, their drivenness. What competitiveness, what demonic compulsion, motivated such grandiose displays of leadership? There is no question that public ministry and leadership are what is required of us in these dangerous times, but combine those virtues with heroism and hubris, and you have a siren calling you to the rocks. You have mediocrity in the making. You have marijuana distorting your perceptions. You have a cancer eating you up on the inside. A terrible toll is exacted from your mortal body.

At first I withdrew into the inner recesses of the ship. I had my ear to the radio and kept up day by day with the war. I was not really surprised by how our new government leaders had let their newly acquired wealth and power get to their heads. The movie I was watching was all too predictable. Loud was the dissent of some of our most respected national thinkers, who urged restraint, self-examination, and addressing the roots of the poverty and alienation of the masses in the Palestinian territories, Saudi Arabia, Iran, Yemen, Pakistan, and Afghanistan, but the new powers turned a deaf ear to them.

The voice came to me again saying, Cry, but I was running and running and running in the opposite direction from Ninevah, from the gravitational pull of its military might and its pervasively demoralizing culture of fear. Several leaders of the congregation had ties to the armed forces, and

I was aware of my own foreign roots, my accent, my skin. Had it not been for the Sunday morning theology group that we had been building up for three years, I may not have come up on the deck easily.

The persons in that group were witty, well-informed women and men of stature who rose above old age and frenetic schedules to gather at nine on Sunday mornings in the old chapel room with a fireplace. The dialogue and friendship and trust had nurtured us all, and we digressed again and again into discussing the invasion of Iraq and its consequences. I am thankful to you, Mike, Sally, and Ruth, for leading the way in opposing the nation's military posture in the actual hearing of the mammoth Darth Vader planes roaring in and out of the airforce base close by. You became my mentors while I was pastor there. I followed in your footsteps and found my suppressed voice, and I preached some of my best and bravest sermons above the commotion in the air and the general pandemonium of war. I do best, fellow travelers, when I am not alone.

31

Landour

*I walk tall on Main Street in the
May Day parade*

TERRORISM HAS MULTIPLIED AND the consumeristic economy is still championed by the best and the brightest. Our sins have received their wages in alienation and anxiety. Catherine Keller's *Face of the Deep* brought some relief. While the sentences dart about in the sea of a new-fashioned jargon, some assertions leap out like dolphins. The chaotic waters of creation do not invite romance, warns the book, and they will not cease to destroy us. But we will not be born, or born again, from any other matrix.

And kudos to Keller for urging, Do not try to control what is out of control, but rather brood upon its waters. Somewhere between what is too chaotic and what is too limiting lies the creative edge. That comforting admonition gave me permission to still surf the sea of ambiguity rather than be a hermit martyr to perfection. In his *Modern Times* Bob Dylan too sings, "Spirit on the water, darkness on the face of the deep/ I keep thinking 'bout you, baby, and I can't hardly sleep." And in *Friendly Fire* John Lennon's son Sean also sings of waiting for someone somewhere out there between the moon and the sea.

Fellow pilgrim, we have come to the end of my story. In this rural town I serve a small church on a part-time basis in my retirement. I listen in the evenings over public radio to the Los Angeles, Chicago, San Francisco, New York, and Amsterdam philharmonic orchestras. I also keep up on the news, and I hear the names of Pakistani cities, Peshawar, Quetta,

Landour

Rawalpindi, Lahore. They are familiar to me from when I was a boy in Ferozepore, which is just across the border, the Sutlej River, from Lahore. Arriving on those famous trains my aunts and uncles brought news at Christmas about the Khyber Pass, the Pathan area, and those faraway Rudyard Kipling places on the northwestern frontier. Some of the local families we knew in the Railway Hospital were in fact from those faraway places too. They were our friends, and I played with their children. I heard somewhere that during the bloody Partition, our family helped some Muslim families reach the border safely.

Even after the Partition I had friends in all castes. We played in the winter when I was home from the mountains. Raj and Bhaji went to school every morning. Their family had a goat. Kishori and Tida belonged to the lowest caste, known until Gandhi came as the Untouchables. He called them Harijans, children of God. The hospital doctor was a Sikh. His son and I walked near the garden in the evening and whispered secret things about a queen out of ancient lore. The white sheep dog Prince was with us, and he was in New Delhi too when I left for America. I loved him and took him with me to Connaught Place, and I would pick him up when we crossed a street. He and I grew close. I often wonder, sadly, what happened to him after I left.

Here I am able to live a relatively earth-friendly lifestyle. In the comfort of the peace group of retired Brethren pastors and others I walk tall on the double yellow lines on Main Street in the festive May Day parade, which includes floats and horses and marching bands from all over the county. Thousands line the street, and I am aware both of the color of my skin and of the peace sign I hold up. People gaze at us out of curiosity and some cheer in support as we pass. They wonder whether this anomalous group is for real.

The exuberance of this march panders to my fantasy of being a larger-than-life comic book superhero in superlative alignment in all my parts. No, I cannot lift up automobiles, and no, I cannot break chains. Nor am I a Joseph Campbell world hero. I have never entered a dark forest to slay dragons, never climbed the high Himalayan passes to visit remote Buddhist monasteries, and never returned from any decisive victory to save the world. Instead, I rise and fall. Sin and Death are still my constant companions, Sin with its fangs and dagger eyes and slimy body the color of the black-water of the sewer, and Death with its pale coiled body and big fanged jaws waiting to devour the weakened victim. They are still beside me as I walk those yellow double lines.

Attractions and jealousies crowd into my soul. Nobody on Main Street sees my invisible companions. No one knows the agitations in Kurukshetra, the irresolution, the unfulfilled desires. We will resolve the conflicts, we will fulfill your cravings, we will round things off when you get home. It is the voice of Sin. The tyranny of this raucous carnival, the drudgery of the church's rummage sale, and the oppressive long lines for the corndogs will pass. At sundown you will be hidden behind the veil of darkness.

Come Sunday morning, however, and a new and opposing music is heard, bursting my prison. I awaken and am already swept into the Forgiveness of this bright dawn. The hymns declare the discipline of Goodness and the readings resound with the practice of Righteousness and Lovingkindness. We soar on the wings of this sacred morn to the skies of Truth and Nonviolence. We sail on the ocean waves of worship to the invisible shoreline of Transcendence and Freedom.

We have a Sunday morning kitchen table theology group at nine in this church too. We gather before the service to companion and support one another in our personal journeys, and we dialogue about how the texts intervene in our driven worlds. This nurtures Honesty, Patience, and the Art of Listening, and it helps me, in particular, stay connected and give fresh sermons, which I have spent the prior week preparing. Strife, wrath, and burning desire withdraw in the brightness of this joyous sunrise, illuminating everything that there is.

Come Sunday morning and prayers go forth for Peace in the Middle East, Iraq, Afghanistan, Darfur, on our own nation's streets, and in our families and personal lives. We lift to the Light the sick, the grieving, the frail, the addicted, and the oppressed, mentioning names. The sermons proclaim the prophetic principle, urging the congregation to do Justice, love Kindness, and walk as one who is Poor in Spirit. They hammer out Respect and Wholeness for all beings all over the land, knowing that all beings, human and nonhuman, participate in Life itself, Creative Power, God. They ring out the interconnectedness of all things, that to Love any being at all is to Love God, and to live in ecological Community with the earth and its creatures is to live in Community with God.

The bread we break is the bread of Infinite Strength, and the cup we pour is the Living Water that leads to Abundant Life.

Landour

Come Sunday morning I again make the long walk to the church across waterways in the park and past cedars with their icy-blue berries, my sermon in my pocket, the sunrise at my back, and the thrumming of woodpeckers in the wind. In the early spring I see through the blowing snow the green blade rising, and my heart takes delight in the rapture of this walk, even when there is murmuring and ill will on the part of at least one layperson in the church. I recall what a church leader had said some years ago about the poisoning of the community well. It takes just one person to say, Are not the sermons getting worse? The new couple doesn't do a thing. Are we really getting our money's worth from the pastor? I push these thoughts aside for another day.

I feast my eyes on the fields of the Great Plains, the fields of passing storms, the fields of the earth in shining splendor, the fields of blowing snow and drifting snow, and the beckoning trees beyond. Fields where the great red sea of eastern clouds appears at dawn on the true horizon.

One night a while ago the field was bright with snow, the Milky Way had occupied the mist, and there was no need for lamp or moon. The faraway lights in the windows were like a Welcome Home for someone long gone.

Fields of victory, fields of defeat, fields of valor. Fields where the weight of the world hinges on you like a theorem. I think I remember watching the full moon from the train long, long ago. It was stopped not far from Delhi at the small deserted station of Kurukshetra in the dead of night. The moon must have hung over the site of the mythic battle and the teaching by the incarnate God Krishna of the embodied soul. Gandhi's assassin had sworn falsely at the bridge. He was hanged somewhere near here, where the ghosts of the slain mocked him. A solitary vendor went by chanting, *Garm chai, Garm chai*, Hot tea, Hot tea, dark against the moon.

Fields of matter against spirit, of action and inaction. Fields of unknowing, of biding one's time, like the starlings motionless on the larch, waiting for winter to end and the migration north to begin. The winter's end is the promise we are given.

The Truth we possess is derived from the blood of railway junctions, from the sparks of colliding worlds, sacred and profane, hither and yonder, and from the chastisement of extreme minds. It comes to our eyes as much by its absence as by its presence, like the Truth of love. Smaller truths come by earthquake, wind, and fire, but the big Truth comes in the still, small voice.

The Meaning of These Days

Let us go, fellow pilgrims, to Kellogg Church high on Landour's mountain, and I will show you the eternal snows massed across the north rim and the simmering plains far below in Dehra Dun to the south, and we will see leaping langurs, sherpas, and shooting stars. The fog in the monsoons creeps up the wet, leechy valleys. In the days of yore the missionaries learned the native language in the day and came from different directions with their Bibles in the evening to gather and sing classical hymns and sacred songs in that church. Far below in the younger boys' dorm Miss Frances' piano upstairs would gallop deep into the landscape of galaxies and mountain villages and terraced rice paddies in the night. Or was it her cello sweeping the mountains and ravines like an immense midnight bird of prey, I do not now remember.

Then when there was silence and everyone was asleep, the sound of a flute could be heard, as if it had been playing all this time but had been muted by the music upstairs. The flute was high but not shrill, not conquering or coveting. While it was coming, I think, from the servants' quarters just below the dorm, it seemed it was coming from some mysterious and beautiful and peaceable domain ancient and far away, defended only by those wispy notes dancing and spiralling upward to the moon and away into the milky night. The families were gathered around their fires with their hookahs and their goats and were quietly resting. The rice paddies would erode in the monsoon, but would again be rebuilt, and sown in the fall with wheat and barley.

www.ingramcontent.com/pod-product-compliance
Lightning Source LLC
Chambersburg PA
CBHW060823190426
43197CB00038B/2205